Sawdust and Soul

Sawdust and Soul

A Conversation about Woodworking and Spirituality

WILLIAM J. EVERETT
and JOHN W. DE GRUCHY

CASCADE *Books* · Eugene, Oregon

Cascade Books
An Imprint of Wipf and Stock Publishers
199 W. 8th Ave., Suite 3
Eugene, OR 97401

www.wipfandstock.com

ISBN 13: 978-1-62564-463-3

Cataloguing-in-Publication Data

De Gruchy, John W.

Sawdust and soul : a conversation about woodworking and spirituality / William J.
Everett and John W. de Gruchy

xiv + 90 p. ; 23 cm. Includes bibliographical references.

ISBN 13: 978-1-62564-463-3

1. Woodwork. 2. Wood in art. 3. Spirituality. 4. Spirituality in art. 5. Christianity
and the arts. I. Everett, William Johnson. II. Title.

BR115.A8 D42 2015

Manufactured in the U.S.A.   12/05/2014

For Sylvia and Isobel,
without whose encouragement, patient indulgence, and appreciation
we couldn't make the sawdust or lift our souls.

The Conversation

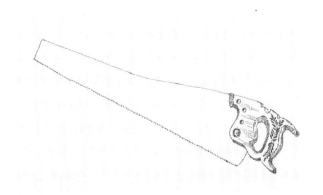

Acknowledgments

Isobel de Gruchy's poem "When I Think Olive" appeared earlier in Isobel de Gruchy, *Walking On: Poems, Prayers, Pictures* (Hermanus, South Africa: published by the author, 2013).

William J. Everett's poem "The Fall" appeared earlier in William J. Everett, *Turnings: Poems of Transformation* (Eugene, OR: Wipf and Stock, 2013).

The drawing of the tulip poplar tree on p. 18 is by Isobel de Gruchy and reproduced here with her permission.

About This Book

We were originally drawn together by our common interest in theology and public life, with me in the United States and John in South Africa. But we soon discovered another deep connection—a love for wood and woodworking. Early on in our friendship when John was visiting us in Boston, we went together to a party in one of the grand old homes near where Sylvia and I lived. All the wood paneling, the floors, and the furniture in the house were made out of cherry. It was a stunning testament to a time of giant trees and elegant craftsmanship. We marveled together about the wood and the craft while others milled about in academic conversation. Our friendship in wood had previously begun one evening in Cape Town the year before. But now it was sealed and our conversation began in earnest.

Over the years since then we have talked off and on about the way working with wood has shaped not only how we work with words, but how we live our lives. Woodworking has been a life-giving complement to our work as academic theologians. Like many others, in our retirement this work of our hands has become a transforming vehicle for discerning what it is to live a life "in the spirit." Woodworking has been essential for navigating our way into this phase of our lives—in my case more as a fresh expression of my previous interests, in John's more as a necessary complement— bringing balance and enabling fresh creativity. So it was that for John's retirement colloquium at the University of Cape Town in May 2003, I presented a paper about woodworking, spirituality, and ethics, in which I lifted up the importance of woodworking for his theological work. Much to the amazement and fascination of his colleagues from around the world, John also displayed, and then we commented on, some of his turned bowls and other outcomes of his woodcraft.

In this little book we share some reflections on the way this life with wood has brought about a broadening and deepening of our own lives. We use our experience not just to craft meditations illustrating previously held convictions, but as an entrance into new understandings, practices, and sensibilities. In doing so, we invite you to join our conversation about the ways woodworking has shaped our "spirituality," our way of being in the world, whether you are an "all thumbs" theologian, a seeker, a pilgrim, or a practical woodworker. We've even included a glossary at the end to help you with any terms with which you may not be familiar, and had some fun in compiling it. While we both speak and write our own form of English, we decided to use American spellings and retain the Imperial measurements of feet and inches, even though we both agree the metric system is far easier for woodworking! But we use both the American "shop" and the British "workshop" to describe the place where we do our woodworking.

We need to make clear that this is *not* a handbook for woodworking. While we describe some of our experiences and techniques, we are not seeking to instruct you in woodworking. For that you can turn to one of the fine books or magazines noted in the bibliography or, if you are so fortunate, to programs at your local schools or woodworking clubs. And please be mindful that while woodworking is a great hobby, it involves sharp tools and machinery. So make sure you take all safety rules seriously.

We'll start with how we got into this craft. Then we'll talk about the way the world of trees that we inhabit has shaped not only us but our whole culture. We then turn to what we have learned from some of our own projects. At the end we'll reflect on how woodworking takes place in communities of relationships between generations and among friends.

Working with wood can be a deeply solitary activity, but it always takes place in relationships—with wood as well as people. Among these are the many associations, clubs, and informal networks that have enabled us to improve our woodworking. There are also many people to thank for this journey—parents and grandparents, wives and sisters, children and grandchildren, colleagues, and friends in wood. You'll hear us talking about our friends who have helped us with their skills, their tools, their shops, and their thoughts about the craft they love. The voices of our children will also enter the conversation as they pick up in their own ways where we leave off. We also want to give a special thanks to Isobel de Gruchy, who has graciously supplied the line drawings of tools that beautify the book's transitions, labored over the production of the photos accompanying the text, and also made some editorial suggestions.

Well, John, let's start talking! The project is waiting. Why don't you kick off and tell us something about your life in woodworking?

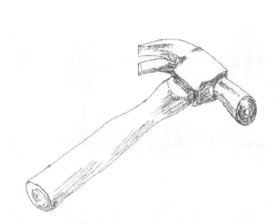

Living with Wood

John's Story

Thanks, Bill. As you know I have just finished a book on my life in writing as an academic that I've entitled *A Theological Odyssey*, so it's about time to share the story of my life in woodworking. Writing, woodworking, and playing sport intersected my life from an early age. As a teenager I dreamt of writing a murder mystery, but I gave up after a few pages. At school I was more interested in cricket and hockey than in Latin and Mathematics. Yet by the time I went to university in my seventeenth year I had taught myself to type and enjoyed writing the essays that from then on became a constant part of my life.

My father Harold always had a workshop. He made the furniture for our first family house, including two large teak Morris Chairs, which I inherited but no longer have. He taught me the basics of woodworking and bought me a second-hand lathe when I was still in junior school. I have no idea what happened to it after I left home. Woodworking was part of the junior school curriculum, at least for boys, so it was there that I was taught elementary industrial drawing and developed my rudimentary woodworking skills. But even though I was not particularly good at either, the smell of boiling horse-hooves glue pellets on the gas burner remains part of my memory, and a pen and inkpot stand I made from mahogany still sits on my study desk.

My younger son Anton would later do woodwork throughout his high school years, and did much better. But, alas, woodworking is no longer an option in the vast majority of schools in South Africa, including those to which we went. This is an enormous pity and loss, as has been the demise of the apprenticeship system. There are signs that both will be re-introduced, something that cannot come quickly enough. To learn to use your brain in the school room and your muscle on the sports field are obviously important, but so too is learning to appreciate the creative arts and crafts that add such value to life and to the community, whether as a profession or hobby. I was fortunate to be introduced to all these at school, and they remain important, giving my life some necessary equilibrium. Developing this balance has become important over the years on my journey into becoming more fully human and, in the process, nourishing my soul.

Although I have always had my own workshop since Isobel and I were married and, from time to time, made furniture and other items needed for our various homes over the years, woodworking increasingly took a back seat as my work in a congregation, my involvement in public life, and my life as an academic (and much travel), took centre stage. It was not only woodworking that suffered; I fear that amidst everything else I could not have been a very good father. But Steve and Anton got something of their own back, for my workshop became a bicycle repair shop (their sister Jeanelle was party to some of their exploits as well, though she now denies it!), and the chisels I had once kept sharp were put to uses other than those for which they were intended.

Life was difficult, hectic, and sometimes fearful during the final years of the struggle against apartheid in which our whole family, many colleagues and friends, as well as our local church, were engaged in one way or another. But then Nelson Mandela walked out of prison, a new era dawned, and the rest is history, though the journey towards a transformed society is still in its infancy. These dramatic changes affected all of our lives, not least my own, giving us a new freedom. I was able to start research projects that were no longer focused on the church struggle against apartheid, though still usually related to Christian faith and public life. But as the 1990s progressed it was becoming clear—at least to Isobel, if not to myself—that the intensity of the previous years had taken its toll on soul and spirit as well as body. And the gusto with which I was now involved in new writing projects was not helping to restore the balance so necessary for a meaningful and productive life.

I vividly recall the day on which Isobel told me in no uncertain terms that I had better find a hobby and get my life more in balance. She was right. But my workshop was a shambles, my tools rusty and blunt, and my skills, such as they were, all but forgotten. Yet, after a moment's reflection—it took not much longer—I resolved to return to my workbench, rescue my chisels, and make sawdust again. I don't think Isobel had a clue as to what this would mean—or cost, for that matter—when she encouraged me to buy new tools and get going again, or in terms of the time I would devote to doing so. But she was delighted, not least because at the same time she was developing her own skills as an artist and poet after years of doing community work and teaching school mathematics. We were both in search of a more balanced life as we began to think ahead to the so-called years of "retirement," a notion that could mean becoming bored to death, or alive to new possibilities. Fortunately we had the resources to avoid the former and pursue the latter. In that regard we are privileged, but also enormously grateful.

Anton re-introduced me to woodturning during a holiday we spent at the Moffat Mission in Kuruman, on the edge of the Kalahari Desert, where Steve, his older brother, was the director during the 1990s. I was hooked. So one of the first pieces of equipment I bought for my renovated, though small, workshop was a No 1 Record woodturning lathe. Then I had the opportunity, during a sabbatical in England in 1998, not only to write a book on *Christianity and Democracy* but also to attend a woodturning course given by Alan Batty in the Yorkshire cathedral town of Ripon. He helped me get the basics more or less right, but he was also a stickler for perfection. I am not sure he regarded me as amongst his better pupils, but I undoubtedly benefitted from his tuition. On another occasion I took a course in wood carving in the English Peak District, and although I have not done much carving since then (a few pieces are the exception), it was a good experience. I cannot recommend strongly enough to anyone keen to get started in woodcraft that you find a mentor. On our return to Cape Town from our sabbatical in England I resolved to enlarge my workshop, buy a bigger lathe with a swinging headstock to turn large bowls, and join a woodturning club.

Around that time, my brother-in-law, Ron Steel, who had long been my companion in various ventures, retired from the ministry, and with his wife Elsie and family came to live in Cape Town. Ron was an avid woodworker and was also beginning to develop an interest in woodturning. So together we joined the Pinelands Club and twice a month for several years participated in its meetings. What a learning experience that was! We were introduced to tools and techniques, watched and shared in practical demonstrations, rubbed shoulders with some remarkable turners, marveled at their skill and output, entered competitions, received excellent critique, and even progressed to what was designated an "advanced level" of woodturning. Above all, we became passionate wood turners. And I also learned that some things had changed since the days of shop class.

Having learnt much from feminist theologians over the years, I suppose I shouldn't have been surprised when towards the end of our sojourn in the Pinelands Woodturners club several women joined and soon established themselves as accomplished turners. I know that sounds patronizing, for why should they not excel at woodturning as at everything else? I suppose it is just because woodworking has always seemed such a men's thing, something like rugby and cricket! But seeing that there are now women's rugby and cricket teams, why not wood turning? The circle has turned, and none too soon. I am sure it started in the US before it did in South Africa. In fact, I now recall that several years before women joined the Pinelands club, I visited a craft festival in Hyde Park, Chicago, where I met a woman turner whose exquisite work inspired me. Be that as it may, I owe much to that club in Pinelands and to Ron's companionship along the way. Ron himself later managed a large solid wood furniture factory and continues to make fine furniture as a hobby. Children establishing a home are very fortunate beneficiaries of such a father's craftsmanship!

Then you entered my workshop. While we had originally talked of collaborating on our research in Cape Town that year, I ended up taking my sabbatical in England, while you and Sylvia stayed in our house. But it only took one evening before we left for us to discover that our interests extended well beyond doing theology; we also shared a passion for woodworking, and a zany sense of humor—something very necessary both in friendship and in the workshop.

Over the succeeding years, as you and I have moved into "retirement," we have found every opportunity we can to share our woodworking interests together, whether during your visits to Cape Town or Volmoed, where we now live, or ours to your home in Waynesville, North Carolina, a part of the United States, which is a Mecca for woodworkers. As I write this piece, I am looking at the bookcase we made on one occasion for my study, which now houses my Bonhoeffer collection—another passion. Above, on the veranda overlooking the valley below, are two Adirondack chairs we made on your most recent visit, with some help from Serghay van der Bergh, about whom I will say more later. And now we are busy writing together—but writing about woodworking, and in the process making connections with our journeys into theology, social ethics and public life, and the nurturing of soul.

In thinking about our lives in woodworking and those of others who have inspired and guided us, I guess we have come to distinguish woodworkers by their skills and the kind of work they do. Some are carpenters who do essential work in building homes, others are furniture makers whose skills are similar but not the same, for they do more refined work in order to produce items that are both functional and beautiful. Then there are the cabinetmakers. These are the saints of woodworking, those we reverently read about in *Fine Woodworking* magazine and whose work is a marvel to behold. I am nowhere near that end of the spectrum, nor would I regard myself as a maker of fine furniture, but I am inspired by those who set the pace, just as I am by the witness of those who courageously struggle for justice and peace, or those whose spiritual depth, compassion, and insight enrich and challenge us all.

It strikes me that the difference between good and bad craftsmanship is not unlike the one between good and bad religion. It is not the discrepancy between the simplicity of a Shaker chair or the elegance and beauty of a Restoration cabinet, but between a shoddy piece of work and one that has integrity. We need saints, whether of the spirit or the craft, to remind us of that difference and that there are still mountains to climb. But, as you would remind me, we can't all be saints, and there is forgiveness for failures; in fact, a mistake at the workbench can often lead to an exciting new creation. Woodworking, after all, is meant to bring happiness and delight, not sadness and despair. Knowing that helps when you get tired and cut your fingers, when lovely wood is butchered or sawdust overwhelms the soul, or when tempted to throw in the towel and confine our failures to the firewood pile. Writer's block and woodworker's frustration are much the same. When the joy goes out of what you are doing, shut up shop for a while, watch a movie or go for a walk. But get back to the laptop and bench as soon as you can.

One of the joys in "retiring" to Volmoed, a Christian retreat centre nestling among the hills and vineyards of the Hemel en Aarde Valley near Hermanus, is that we were able to build our own house—designed by Julian Cooke, a great architect and friend over the years—and include in it plans for a large workshop. This has become a wonderful sanctuary over the past decade. Not only is it big enough to include all my tools and machines, but also large enough for at least two people to work together in it on various projects such as you and I have undertaken. In it, Ron has taught me to turn segmented bowls and Anton helped me build the staircase banisters in our house and the extensive bookshelves in my library. To share such a passion with friends, relatives, or children is very special and I still look forward to more opportunities to come.

Serghay has been a more frequent companion in the workshop. He is a younger member of the maintenance staff on Volmoed who has taken a special interest in woodworking and has become my unofficial "apprentice" during periods in his schedule when he is able to join me. I learn as much from him as he does from me. After all, he has built his own house! He also has no compunction in reminding me about the safety rules we have

established, on measuring twice before cutting, and striving for perfection when tempted to cut a few corners.

My life in writing and woodworking! How fulfilling this has all been. But it is also an expression of something deeper that has to do with the work of the spirit of creativity, inspiration, empowering, and aesthetic awareness. The truth is, my life-long journey in the church, academy, and public life have become inseparable from the workshop, giving my life added meaning, enjoyment, nourishment, and direction. This is, I have come to believe, the work of the Spirit, whose activity is not confined to religion or to the soul (understood as some rarefied ghost in the machine we call the body), but embraces life in all its dimensions, relationships, joys, and sorrows, and crosses boundaries of time and space. In the process, sawdust flies in all directions, but the soul also takes wings.

∾

Bill's Story

Ah, John, the chips and sawdust are inspiring you to poetry! There are so many similarities in our stories, but also some different paths as well. Unlike you I grew up among trees, but not among woodworkers. Washington, DC was filled with trees among its low buildings. Living on its edge, I roamed an abandoned farm at the end of our street, trapping squirrels (don't ask), ripping out the surveyors' stakes (yes, I have a criminal past), and constructing lean-tos and tree platforms from the branches available on the ground. At one point I built an underground fort (being a youth, I called it a fort), only to discover that it flooded in heavy rains. Stick to tree houses, at least till lightning hits.

At most, wood was a construction material for the barns, fence-posts, and houses on the family's dairy farm in Virginia where I spent all my non-school time. I got to know wood as locust, oak, pine, and maple. My father (a William Jr., with me being a third) was a businessman, and at best a tinkerer and repairman. In those days being the "third" meant you would follow in your ancestors' footprints, but obviously I didn't. Through wood I first learned what it was to repair things. A farm, I came to say, is a repair waiting to happen, whether it is a broken fence or a hole in the shed roof.

But there was one exception to this strictly utilitarian view of wood. When I was thirteen I too was introduced to the world of woodcraft through my school's Shop Class. That it was strictly offered for boys did not strike me as strange either. Boys were supposed to work with heavy materials. Girls were supposed to sew, cook, and run the household. That we would soon live in a world where this made no sense was an unacknowledged corrosive that finally did away with shop and home economics. Only recently have these enterprises begun to reappear in the schools as tools for living that are open to both girls and boys. Like you, I have seen the emergence of fine woodworkers and turners like Laura Mays at the College of the Redwoods, Dixie Biggs, or Betty Scarpino, who is also editor of *American Woodturner*, by the way. And there are many others.

It was in Shop Class that I discovered sophisticated tools (for that era) like the router, the lathe, and the metal press. I don't remember the teacher's name, a man with gruff demeanor and sure hands, intent on passing on his skills to boys who didn't really know what shop skills were for, but who loved the chance to take some wood and change it into bookends, bowls, and magazine racks.

My magazine rack was made of mahogany or something close to it. After residing for some decades with my parents, it returned to me upon their deaths. A few years ago I coaxed it apart—we used water-soluble hide glue then, no fancy aliphatic glues— and repaired some damaged joints. There were the old mortises I had made with a router that must have sounded like a freight train. Cleaned out, some edges repaired, and the rack stood ready once again to house the magazines I can't bear to throw out after they are read. It held a lot of *National Geographics* until I started giving them to my son Eric.

The magazine rack reminds me that wood is a potent vehicle of memory. It is like an ancient ancestor who remains among us, reminding us of stories that are the backbone of our own development. Objects of wood also remind us as human beings that we are people of the trees, primordial workers of wood, creatures whose unity of hand and mind make us what we are.

While I went on to live increasingly through my world of ideas, language, and speech, the intense satisfaction of my experience in those shop classes remained with me, tugging at me as I emerged into a career of teaching, writing, and public speech. I had little awareness that many of the craft values realized in shop were also guiding the way I wrote, thought, and engaged in the administration of academic affairs.

My only effort in woodwork took place in my mid-twenties, when I constructed an elaborate stand for the sound equipment and records that had accumulated in my collegiate and graduate school years. Made of numerous slats and threaded rods, with one diagonal bracer board, it was designed to be taken apart for the many moves of a scholar's early life. Needless to say, it was so intricate I only disassembled it under dire need. I finally passed it on to a friend and it disappeared from my life, a fleeting testimony to ingenuity and the paucity of tools, space, and resources at my disposal. But I was helping raise three kids, too, who have reminded me that I engaged in enough woodworking during those years to pass on some skills and attitudes.

Eric, a Star Trek fan at age seven, remembers how we built a small closet in his bedroom that was the base of a rocket ship, with a painted façade, a control room, and all sorts of Wizard-of-Oz controls. It was, he says, his first stage set. He went on to major in theater in college and has spent much of his career designing and building stage sets. Of course, he says, "I don't have to be as concerned about how it looks close up!"

My daughter Aneliese tells me that my matter-of-fact involvement of her in my projects taught her confidence with tools and habits of work that she has carried into her work in graphic arts and jewelry design. I really never thought about these things. It was just the way we did things together. "Always productive," she would add with a grin.

At one point in those interim years there emerged a very small, seemingly insignificant symbol of the meaning of woodworking in my life. It was a time, as Dante said, that I came to an impasse—"a dark wood"—in my life. My usual guides had fallen away and I couldn't see how to link the story of my past to a viable future. It was then that I took a small piece of wood—pine or spruce—and carved a small boat as a symbol of the unknown journey ahead, a journey that took me to a new life with my beloved Sylvia and a developing new understanding of my vocation. Wood was not only a vehicle of memory but of hope and transformation. These themes have been at the heart of much of my life and work ever since—themes that have pressed with persistent nudging to a deeper work with wood as well as words.

It was only when we built our retirement home, complete with a large basement blasted out of our mountainside in the Smokies, that I was able to start assembling the machines, workbenches, and shelves that would become the workshop I have worked in for the last twenty years. The extra cost of a full basement was one of the best investments I've ever made.

~

The Enchantment of Trees

It was for me, too, Bill. And it's fortunate that both of us live surrounded by trees. Your home, high up on the slopes of the Appalachians above Waynesville, is located in a forest of cherry, walnut, and maple. Our home is built on a ridge looking down the Hemel en Aarde Valley, near Hermanus, a coastal town 100 miles southeast of Cape Town, widely known as the whale capital of the world. Next to our house is a small forest of tall pine and eucalyptus trees that link earth and heaven. From our deck you can see many more trees on every side, stretching over the farm and down the valley, trees of every shape and size, with leaves of many shades of green—eucalyptus, plane, oak, camphor, yellow-wood, wild olive, cottonwood, keurbooms, poplars, boekenhout, waterberry alders, and the ubiquitous invasive aliens, pines, bluegums, and Port Jackson willows. It is not a case of us not seeing the wood for the trees; when we see the trees we already have a sense of what lies hidden behind the bark and the outer rings of sapwood. We discern the heart wood deep within that gives the furniture we make its quality, texture, and rich colors.

Many years ago, when I was a graduate student in Chicago living in Hyde Park, I noticed one of my professors, Ross Snyder, walking past our window on the sidewalk. He suddenly stopped in front of a tree, I forget the kind, and then, so it seemed, he began talking to it. I was dumfounded, and even more so when later I found out that he was, indeed, having a conversation! I no longer think he was a little peculiar. Thomas Pakenham, in his wonderful books *Meeting with Remarkable Trees* and *Remarkable Trees of the World* tells about his many encounters with trees across the globe, including South Africa where he has spent much time.

•

John, the story of Ross Snyder reminds me that the sermon I gave as a senior at Yale Divinity School was entirely a soliloquy directed at the large maple outside the windows flanking the chapel. In talking to the tree, as in later years I talked to a large bowl of dirt (that's another story!), I was entering into the world of associations we have with trees, as well as reifying in some sense their very mystery, their very otherness. If Ross and I are crazy,

at least we aren't alone! We both have acted into the ancient mystery of the
tree.

•

Ancient and yet very personal, Bill. And we owe our life to them. I
am told that the first trees began to evolve 300 million years ago and within
another 100 they covered the earth as the most successful plants of all. They
also live longer than any other living organism on the planet. They are fundamental to life, they provide food, and their wood can be used in many
different ways. In short, they are an amazing part of the plant kingdom, so
varied and complex in kind, in shape and size, in texture and color, that it
is almost impossible to classify them with complete accuracy. But once you
start working with wood, you need to get to know trees, the strengths and
weaknesses of their wood for the tasks at hand, and how best you can help
them begin their new life whatever that might be.

For instance, the trees in the Appalachians are wonderful for furniture making. I envy you going out of your shop into the forest to select
a tree for your next project. When I look at them I see order, stateliness,
clear lines, regular patterns, straight grain, consistent color, and can already
imagine a cabinet or table that would grace any mansion. I love working
with such wood, along with ash, beech, white and red oak, mahogany, teak,
rosewood—but all of these have to be imported into South Africa at con-
siderable expense. So I shudder in alarm when you feed off-cuts into your
woodstove! I take comfort that you live in the middle of a forest that continually replenishes itself, fed by abundant water and rich soil. Our climate
and depth of soil, by contrast, varies greatly from one end of the country
to the other. It can't nurture and sustain forests on such a scale. With a few
exceptions, the Knysna forest being one, we have nothing as extensive as
those that stretch along the Appalachian Mountains or the Cascades and
Rockies in North America.

All the trees on Volmoed are strikingly textured and colorful, but are
individually precious for their beauty and shade, and have not grown without a struggle. I marvel how each tree has its own character and seems to be-
long to the place where it has taken root, even if imported from elsewhere.
These trees are seldom available for my workshop, unless blown over in a
storm, and only a few can be turned, carved, or used for furniture. Most do
not grow straight, but are gnarled and shaped by wind and weather, by their
varied genes, and by their location on the farm. As we live in the midst of
the Fynbos kingdom, one of the six floral kingdoms in the world, we have

to work hard to control invasive species. We have an ongoing struggle to eradicate them, or at least control them. They provide wood to make charcoal and logs to burn for warmth and cooking, but are not much value in my workshop. Pine and meranti aside, when I need wood for special projects I hasten to my favorite timber merchants appropriately named "Rare Woods" in Cape Town or "Exotic Woods" in Hermanus. Blackwood, stinkwood, oak, African rosewood or walnut, Brazilian peppercorn, cedar, balau, imbuia, kiaat, jacaranda, and camphor are the ones I love to work with most, but some are now difficult to obtain, others are listed as invasive aliens by government and cannot be planted, many are increasingly expensive, not least because we have mismanaged and abused them for far too long. So you and I are amongst the growing numbers of people who oppose the wanton destruction of forests, and try to ensure that the wood we use in our workshops is harvested sustainably.

The truth is, without trees there is no life. Trees turn carbon dioxide into oxygen, without which we cannot survive. They provide fruit that nourishes us, medicines that heal us, shade that protects us, wood to heat our homes, beams for our roofs, and planks for our doors and floors. Without trees we would only have plastic chairs and tables and metal bookcases. Without trees there would have been no boats and ships, and as my forebears arrived in South Africa from Europe by sailing ship, as did your pilgrim ancestors in New England, we would not be where we are without sturdy oak timber. Without trees there would be no pencils and paper, no baseball or cricket bats, and no wood from which to turn bowls or make furniture. Perish the thought! Even alien trees provide firewood for those in deep rural areas without electricity and are of use in many other ways. And, until the recent evolution of digital books, without trees there would be no books, including this one. The list of the roles trees play in our lives may not be endless, but it is remarkably extensive. No wonder we should care for the trees and strike up a better relationship with them.

And I know, from what you said about your early sermon, one of those relationships is really a sacred one. After all, trees figure prominently in most religious traditions as they do in the Bible. They demarcate sacred space as well as have symbolic significance. The Buddha was enlightened beneath the Bo tree. In the Psalms trees shout for joy and clap their hands. Jesus likened people to trees that bear good and bad fruit, and was eventually crucified on a cross of wood, sometimes also referred to as a tree. In fact, the story of trees runs all through the biblical narrative, not only as an important source of food but also providing symbols for life-giving creativity as well as the seduction of power. "Out of the ground the Lord God made to grow every tree that is pleasant to the sight and good for food, the tree of life also in the midst of the garden, and the tree of the knowledge of good and evil" (Gen 2:4b–9).

According to the Genesis creation myth, God planted many trees in Paradise and invited Adam and Eve to enjoy their fruit. But these two trees take center stage. Adam and Eve are encouraged to eat the fruit of the tree of life, but forbidden that of the tree of the knowledge of good and evil. We can readily understand the first, but the prohibition to eat the fruit that enables us to know the difference between good and evil seems strange. Surely that is a part of our growth towards full maturity? After all, some great theologians, starting with Irenaeus in the second century, interpreted the "Fall of Man" as a necessary stage in human development, so we should not press the metaphor of the tree of knowledge lest we miss the point—humans proudly positioning themselves beyond good and evil as the measure of all things. God tells humans not to eat of its fruit because in doing so they will think they know everything, that they can control and dominate everything, and that they can use everything for their own ends and purposes.

There is another angle that is worth thinking about. The Hebrew words translated "good" and "evil" have a wider reference than the English words. They actually speak of a split in our personalities. If the fruit of the tree of life brings wholeness, the tree of the knowledge of good and evil splits us apart. Pleasure, beauty, and the good can no longer exist without pain, ugliness, and evil. Tasting the fruit of the tree of death injects into our being a tension in which despair battles with hope. If the tree of life heals us because its fruit brings together the disparate parts of life, reconciling them and renewing us, the tree of death plunges us into ambiguities, giving us knowledge that is separated from wisdom. We become incapable of living in freedom and empowered to do the good.

Yes, indeed, our ancestors in faith knew a thing or two about the significance of trees. That is why the tree of life frames the biblical narrative from the opening chapters to the closing ones in the book of Revelation. And in the middle of the story stands the tree on which Jesus was crucified (Acts 5:30). Reserved for the worst of criminals and terrorists, and later blasphemed in the burning of crosses and lynching trees of the Ku Klux Klan, the cross has become a symbol of the tree of life that brings healing and reconciliation to people and nations—thus awakening the hope that in the end all things will be restored and renewed in a new Paradise, as in John's vision in the book of Revelation of the tree whose leaves are for the healing of the nations (Rev 22:2).

There is also a lot in contemporary mythic literature involving trees and the stark struggle between good and evil. In Tolkien's *Lord of the Rings* the Ents protect the forests from the dangerous Orcs. They are tree-like creatures who actually become trees like those they protect. They are powerful creatures who had been taught how to talk by the Elves. So when war broke out between the Elves and the awful tyrant Sauron and his minions, the Ents came to their rescue. The myth of the titanic struggle between the Ents and Elves, on the one side, and the Orcs of darkness led by Sauron, on the other, is symbolic of the struggle between the forces of life—namely the forests—and the forces of death—unrestrained technology, symbolized by the dark mines from which comes the iron ore to make weapons of mass destruction.

The struggle symbolized by trees and wood, on the one hand, and iron and steel, on the other; between the saving of the forests which give life, and their destruction for profit by powerful machines owned by powerful institutions, is the struggle between the use of technology for the good of the earth and its inhabitants, and the abuse of technology for greed and exploitation. The dark forests of older times that symbolized danger for travelers and folk living close by have been replaced by the dark mines at ever-increasing depth that produce precious metal and other minerals at enormous cost, not least of lives, and the metals needed to make the machines of war and terror.

There can be no gainsaying the enormous benefits of science and technology, and the many machines they have made possible. I write on a laptop computer that is more powerful than any that existed when men were first sent to the moon. I would be lost without it. Every time I go to the doctor or the dentist, I rejoice in the advances of medical technology, and I marvel at the way my ISUZU bakkie (what you call a "pickup") keeps going. I gladly embrace the speed and ease of global travelling, despite the hassles of airports and the size of the seats. And all the machinery in my workshop is the outcome of advances in woodworking technology, even the hand tools that many a woodworker cherishes. Yes, I am a fan of science and technology, and I confess that I daily add to the carbon footprint that endangers the world. So I need to remind myself constantly—for the sake of my soul, if nothing else—that technology makes weapons, harmful drugs, and pollutes the earth. Ah, yes, and what about turning wood into massive clouds of carbon monoxide? That is why I return again and again to ponder the wonderful myth of Paradise.

Every day as I wake up and look down the Hemel en Aarde Valley, this tree-filled vision comes to mind and feeds my soul. But even this daily reminder did not prepare me for a recent visit to a mythically charged and mysterious "enchanted forest" that lies a few miles away over the distant hills. I couldn't wait to tell you all about it, because it embodied in splendid fashion our conviction that learning to love trees helps us recover a sense of the mystery of soul and the mystery that enfolds us and which we call God.

So here's the story of our visit. Less than an hour's drive from Volmoed, hidden behind the hills above Stanford and Gansbaai, lies a beautiful valley. And in that valley is a forest of indigenous trees named Platbos—an Afrikaans word meaning "flat woods or forest." An information pamphlet describes it in this way: "Platbos is a mystery forest. Growing upon an ancient sand dune with neither a river nor spring to sustain it, the forest survives the hot, dry summer months by drawing moisture from the morning mists that bathe its thirsty canopy." Numbered amongst its trees is a milkwood reputed to be a thousand years old. On the surrounding hills fynbos flourishes, and invasive aliens struggle for control. But in this enchanted forest above a sand dune with neither a river nor a spring to sustain it, indigenous trees grow and flourish.

I don't know the botanical names of the trees in the forest, but let me mention their popular names and how they are described by those who lovingly manage Platbos and extract their essences. The milkwood is the tree of wholeness; the white pear, the tree of joy; the rock alder, the tree of bliss; the bladder nut, the tree of self-knowledge; the wild peach, the tree of courage; the hard pear, the tree of forgiveness; the spike thorn, the tree of loving kindness; the saffron wood, the tree of tears; the sea guarrie, the tree of inspiration; the wild olive, the tree of faith; the pock ironwood, the tree of intuition; the cherry wood, the tree of serenity; and the white stinkwood, the tree of light. Their names, let alone their smells, conjure up a world of mystery and enchantment.

Platbos reminded me that forests are the stuff of fairy tales and legends. In olden times, they were the boundaries between villages, and most villagers seldom ventured alone into their foreboding darkness. They were places where danger lurked, strange things happened, monsters hid, aliens dwelt, and big bad wolves ate straying boys and girls. It was not impossible, as C. S. Lewis once said, that an ogre might live less than an hour away! But Platbos is not a place to fear, it is a place to be renewed, to regain a sense of proportion, a place to discover oneself and share with others your deepest thoughts. You can walk through its shaded paths, sit under its trees, marvel at its shapes and forms, and sometimes on a moonlit night you might even see a shy leopard seeking its prey, or a striped genet clinging to the branches of a stinkwood tree.

It is true that the Old Testament prophets sometimes identified enchanted forests or sacred groves with idolatry, superstition, and sorcery, yet for Ezekiel and some of the psalmists, trees also provided metaphors for the renewal of life, anticipating the day when the trees of the forest would clap their hands and sing for joy (Ps 96:12). Or as St. Paul puts it, the whole creation groans in expectation of a humanity that has come to its senses and begun to care for it with renewed love and energy (Rom 8:22).

We are fortunate to be living in an age today when people across the globe are seeking to reclaim the enchanted forests that are so necessary for life in its fullness, protesting against the greed that destroys the trees that renew the very air we breathe. For we have come to see that if you rid the world of its enchanted forests and all that they symbolize as well, you rid it of the essences of life. So it is not surprising that there is a hankering for places of enchantment to which we can retreat in search of solitude and the renewing of soul. This is not naive romanticism; it is the recognition that we need such places and spaces for the sake of retaining our humanity and renewing our souls. A walk in an enchanted forest can lead us deeper into the mystery of the incarnate God through whom "all things have been created," and "in [whom] all things hold together." Which reminds me of an intriguing verse in the *Gospel of Thomas*, the most important of the apocryphal gospels from the first centuries of Christianity. It is a saying of Jesus: "Raise the stone, and there you will find me; cleave the wood, and there I am" (77). It was probably excluded from the New Testament because it seemed to support the idea that everything is God, what we call pantheism. It is also a reminder that the Spirit of God is the energy that pervades and gives life to the whole of creation. After all, the whole earth is the Lord's and everything in it is a sacrament of God's beauty and love. No wonder the trees of the forest clap their hands and sing for joy.

~

Wounded Whole

The Platbos story resonates a great deal with me, John, because you might say I live in an almost mythical forest, right on the edge of the Pisgah National Forest, abutting the Shining Rock Wilderness. We live in the presence of one of the largest tulip poplar trees in the state of North Carolina. Almost twenty feet around at its base, reaching up over a hundred feet and an equal span across, it sings out the changing seasons on our mountainside. We are not its owners. We are only temporary guardians. Our arborist guesses that its age is over two hundred and fifty years—older than the US Constitution. Cherokee ancestors hunted underneath it, an orchard stretched beneath it until only a few years ago. Until we built our driveway a small spring emerged beneath it. There is a hollow at its base and we surmise it escaped the lumberjacks because of the damage caused by a thunderbolt long ago.

Many of us have some important trees in our lives. They are part of our planet's lungs, source of the very air we breathe. And, of course, they are festooned with religious meanings, from the tree of Eden's paradise to the tree of Revelation's new heaven and new earth. As you said, the more we realize our symbiosis with trees, the more we can be energized to bring our life back in balance with its very source.

The tree became a symbol of one of the first steps I took toward trying to get more balance in my own life. It was 1999. I was asked to give a brief talk at my seminary about faith, healing, and spirituality—not exactly my field—but I accepted. At the time, as I looked out my study window at the tulip poplar, my feet were hurting and my back was all knotted up like a twisted cedar that's been in the wind too long. I really hurt, so I couldn't split those locust logs or work on the stone retaining wall I had so carefully designed during faculty meetings.

Having used up all my Calvinist stoicism I finally called my doctor. He told me I had *plantar fasciitis*. All I could think is that my feet must have acquired some fascist tendencies. Furthermore, he intoned, standing around in Atlanta lecturing when I should have been lying under the tulip poplar had thrown my back out. He said he'd send me an instructional brochure. And try not to walk too much.

Immediately people started crawling out of the woodwork like Job's friends—telling their stories, sharing their remedies, exercises, names of massage therapists and recipes for herbal remedies, some of them containing ginseng or bourbon. The massage therapist was really great. She wore bib overalls, which made me feel comfortable. Her hands were very strong but I trusted her.

The tree told me: Now you might learn something—about roots that don't hit the ground right, about lightning, and about how to live because you have a hollow spot inside. You might even have a shot at wisdom. When you give that talk to those seminary people, remind them about the lightning in their life, about the things that hurt where they touch life's ground, about the hollow places that spare us from ourselves, that let us live.

And you can tell them about what it means to have people come from thousands of miles away to cut you into pieces. They love to cut everything into little pieces—minds, bodies, souls, spirits, knowledge, land, work, time, and space. And then they send the pieces all over the world in order to put things back together in a different way. So that things and living creatures are all split up commuting, connecting, networking, hurrying every which way.

At that point I broke in with my burning question: But why do my feet hurt?

Then I heard the tulip tree say: They hurt because they aren't an instrument. They're you.

The tree was right, of course. How many ancestors had told me that my body was an instrument of my mind, my soul, my spirit? Wesley said: Be useful. Calvin said: Be an instrument of God. And back and back it went. The mind and soul were reasonable, they claimed. The body was a raging beast of passion. Tame it, discipline it, control it.

Over the centuries we came to think of this fleshy instrument as a kind of machine with replaceable parts. And because we thought of our bodies in instrumental terms, we treated those who served our bodies as instruments. And we extended that to all the other creatures in the world as well. And so our world of instruments upon instruments not only can dominate the earth but turns back upon us, subjecting us to a world of mind over matter, of meetings over muscles, schedules over metabolism, typing and tapping over tendons and tissues. Crawling through the labyrinths of bureaucracy, piecing together the fragments of a life on turnpikes and elevators, we feel our muscles knotting, our tendons tearing, our heads splitting. And then there finally comes that painful time when we feel the lightning and touch the hollow that might save us, let us live.

We've reached the limits of our instrumental reason and its tyranny over bodies, nature, people. We are no longer merely an instrument, but now we have the chance to be embodied selves, where feet can talk, backs can cry, and brains can listen. How can we put it? Not instruments, but co-respondents. Respondent to ourselves, respondent to other creatures, to trees and to water, earth and air. Not so much to dominate as to take in and give out. To breathe, to have spirit flowing through our lungs. We're trying to put our life and world back together so it co-responds with the deepest impulses of creation.

And so I gave that talk a few months later. I concluded by saying that I didn't know where this journey was going. Looking back, it was a first step. The tulip poplar was giving me patient permission to begin. It's a very patient tree. It's seen a lot of pain, a lot of cutting, a lot of splendid beauty. And it's still growing, eliciting some poems along the way.

> Wind wrought lightning
>> seared
>> the tulip poplar,

cauterized
    her cambium,
    ripped off her skin,
struck from the pith
    an incensed offering
    to natural wrath.
Yet living on
    she opened grateful leaves
    to rain
    to sun,
received the rings
    of spring's embrace
    around her hollow core,
endures more years
    than our Republic
    wounded
    worthless
    saved from lumberjacks
    and greed.

Now lofty leafed in April
    she greets the sun
    shows off exuberant in May
    slips off her patchwork dress in fall
and waits in winter
    bare-knuckled
    fighting winds
    shaking off the snow
branded
marked
    but unlike Cain
resplendent in the glory
    of God's mercy.

∼

About the Sawdust

We're going to talk a little more about soul later on, Bill, so maybe before we go any further, I should interject some thoughts on sawdust. After all, it's part of the title of this book, and we make lots of it. I'm reminded of a German proverb which reads: "Wo gehobelt wird, da fallen Spähne!" Loosely translated it means that shavings fall to the ground wherever shaving takes place. You can't shave and expect no shavings. I learnt this proverb after a long conversation with our mutual friends Wolfgang and Kara Huber about sawdust—what interesting topics for conversations woodworkers (and even theologians) get into! I mentioned that you and I were writing this book called "Sawdust and Soul." But they didn't know what sawdust meant. So we discussed all the possible German translations and concluded that, as in English, so in German, there are at least two words that can be used. These distinguish between the small specks of dust that result from sawing wood, and the shavings that are made when you plane wood. Of course, when you turn wood on a lathe you get plenty of both because you cut, shave, and sandpaper! Today the up-market vacuum cleaners used in a workshop collect shavings in one bin while the sawdust, being lighter, is sucked into another.

There is an ongoing conversation on the web about how people use sawdust and shavings, some of it quite graphic and not particularly salubrious! Making particle boards and fake snow, providing grip on wet or icy roads, soaking up oil spills, feeding plants, starting a fire, filling wood holes and defects, chasing away weeds, lightening up cement, and providing fuel for boilers. I have also discovered that there is a sawdust art festival, several design studios called "sawdust," someone called the sawdust girl, and even a sawdust mountain, which is described as "a melancholy love letter of sorts," whatever that means! There is also a web page of sentences in which the word "sawdust" occurs. I quote the one I like best: "The unreduced nose of the wine combines figs, apricots, nectarines, scented candle wax, and hard wood sawdust."

Sawdust may have many uses, but it is also toxic. When it gets into your eyes it burns, when it gets into your body it can cause serious allergies, and some is also carcinogenic. It is precisely for this reason that there is such a strong emphasis today in woodworking, especially when using power tools, on the need to wear dust masks, and to suck up sawdust not just from the floor after you have finished working, but as it comes off your machines and before it gets into your lungs. It is not so much the shavings and dust particles you can see that are the problem, but the very tiny specks of dust that float in the air and get into your eyes, your lungs, and, I might add, into your hair as well! So I've learned not to mess with sawdust, it is an irritant and can be a killer. Besides which, Isobel gives me a hard time when I traipse sawdust into the house!

Jesus would have been very familiar with sawdust from working in his father's workshop. So it is not surprising that he uses sawdust as a metaphor when referring to a spiritual blindness that destroys relationships, preventing us from seeing ourselves, others, and the world as we should. But it is, as Jesus also says, nothing compared to having a whole chunk of tree, bark and all, in your eye! "Why do you see the speck in your neighbor's eye, but do not notice the log in your own eye?" he asks his hearers. Jesus is speaking about the danger of judging others—something we are all prone to do, and sometimes do too often for our own and others' good. But the saying could apply more widely. If we have sawdust or logs in our eyes, we not only cannot see the wood for the trees, but we also cannot see the trees. Not only do we fail to see the beauty around us or the good in other people, but we also fail to see the plight of people who suffer from poverty, illness, and old age, or the despair in the eyes of angry unemployed young people. All of which is a reminder of the need to wear safety goggles in the workshop when working with machines to prevent the odd splinter getting into your eyes.

I guess that all this talk about the toxicity of sawdust, and the other dangers lurking in the workshop (and there is more to come!) may well prevent some from venturing in and exploring the possibilities of woodworking or turning for themselves! So maybe we should reassure them that as long as one takes the necessary safety precautions, the workshop is more a place to retreat to for the renewing of spirit than a danger zone housing hazardous power tools! In fact, when the problems of the world get on top of me, I make a beeline for my shop.

Working with Wood

Yes, John, the shop—a potentially dangerous place, but more especially a sacred space. Like the sacred grove, it's not just a place of retreat but of real creativity and renewal. My friend Ed Davis, who says woodworking has kept him sane, tells me he feels that "We honor our Creator when we create." So I guess that makes the shop sacred enough. Now, unlike most churches, mine is cluttered and dusty, always in need of a spring cleaning, for sure! But it's in the shop that I really have a chance for focused work, for concentrating on creating something—or repairing something as well, including ourselves.

Woodchurch

When I got to thinking about this once, a poem sprang up that I'll share here as we talk about the sources of wood and what we need to engage in this craft. For some years I regularly went to meetings of the Carolina Mountains Woodturners Association, one of the largest in the world. Their instructional materials and demonstrations were invaluable to getting me started in turning. When I would leave to drive over to Asheville to the monthly meetings, Sylvia would say, "So you're off to woodchurch today?" Out of her phrase came the title of this poem.

> I have membered
>> and remembered
> God,
>> the ways of God,
>> the hands,
>> the arms,
>> the heart,

in many churches
But their Sundays never could contain
the mystery
that I found in woodchurch,
where the timbers are aligned
to honor grain and knot and figure,
where the beams are tooled with care
and tenoned to perfection,
mortises cut clean in darkness
only God can see.
Among the highest places
boards slip tongues yin yang in grooves,
moving to the rhythm of the seasons,
yielding groans and sighs
with every rising song and organ swell.
In the basement chapel of my woodchurch,
sawdust rises like an incense,
symphonies of saw and chisel,
bit and blade,
sound another offering of praise
to what arises from the earth to touch the sky.

~

The Workbench

Now, Bill, that's a lofty version of our shops! I often marvel at the workshops depicted in *Fine Woodworking* magazine. They are amazingly organized, with not a speck of sawdust in sight. Even the aprons of the woodworkers are spotless; as clean as they possibly could be for a Sunday hour of worship. But can it be for real, knowing full well what goes on in our workshops? At any rate, I am always impressed by the workbenches on display, and am struck by your notion that it is the altar in our woodchurch. Come to think of it, it must be sacred in some sense, because I cannot recall a time before the workbench.

My earliest recollections of my father locate him in his workshop bending over his bench or his lathe. He was a telephone engineer, not a carpenter or turner by trade, but every spare moment he would take off to his workshop. I have already told you that he made all the furniture for the first of our family homes. But he also made my first bench and taught me to plane and saw, and also to turn. Long before I learned to write a school essay, I had learned to work at my bench.

The years I spent at University were benchless. But once installed as pastor of my first congregation in Durban, I made a workbench and bought a new desk, two solid wood companions over the years. I also bought a set of hand tools, and began work on projects for our new home. It would be almost ten years before I had any power tools. A brace and set of bits, a collection of chisels and wooden mallet, some hammers of different sizes, and a rip and tenon saw were my work mates. A member of my congregation added to my collection and provided a load of hardwood from his store, including some wonderful teak.

I recall spending time on my knees as a pastor should, but on one occasion this was in a furniture shop examining the construction of a coffee table Isobel and I admired. Plagiarism did not enter my mind as I later built it out of beautiful solid mahogany given to me by a friend. I eventually gave the table to Steve, and it still serves its purpose in the home of our daughter-in-law Marian in Pietermaritzburg.

Steve, of course, got his own workbench and tools as soon as he was old enough to use them, as did Anton who followed on a few years later. But then came the years in the woodworking wilderness when my bench and tools were used for dubious purposes as Steve and Anton mended their bikes and showed little interest in woodcraft. A "dark night" for the soul of a woodworker! All was not lost, however, for the family genes were at work. Steve eventually became adept at large construction projects—tree houses amongst them. Apart from his theological writing, nothing gave him more pleasure than building in wood, whether on the Moffat mission station in Kuruman, or later in his home in Pietermaritzburg. One of the last things we did together a few months before he died was to build a workbench for his new workshop and equip it more adequately with tools. I now have the occasional pleasure of working on that bench with David, his son, my grandson. Whether or not the bench will become part of his life, I don't know, but I do hope so.

Before Anton and his wife Esther left Cape Town to live and work in Atlanta six years ago, Anton built a fine workbench which is now part of my workshop. But he has built another in his basement shop in Atlanta and has become an excellent woodworker. In fact, as you know, your old lathe is part of his equipment. On our visits to him and Esther we have had good times in his workshop and also in yours in Waynesville, but I have missed his presence in mine. The good news for us is that he and Esther are returning soon to South Africa and will live near us. So I look forward to the years ahead with great anticipation.

I'm certainly glad to know that my workshop will be in safe hands in the future, for one of the saddest days in my life was when I went to fetch my father's tools. He was in his eighties and he and my mother were about to move from their apartment into a senior citizens' home. His work-shop, now only a corner of a small garage, had remained his sanctuary since his retirement. The old bench—his altar—still stood firm and solid, bearing the scars from my own work. The tools were ready to be loaded into my station wagon, including the large wooden toolbox  that was amongst the first things he had made. He was a big man; he still wore his workshop apron. He watched me load the car. I did not take the workbench. It was too large and I had my own. We hugged. I watched him in the rearview mirror as I drove away. There were tears in his eyes. I still wonder where the workbench is. But if it still exists and is in use, no one will know its story. I have never told it before.

Migrating from workbench to desk and back again, from making fur-niture to writing books, has become the rhythm of my life. There is, I think, a symbiotic relationship between them, at least for me. Power tools may have replaced some of my hand tools, and my laptop my old typewriter, but watching planks becoming tables and chairs evokes the same wonder as seeing words develop into sentences and paragraphs into books. This is not surprising. For without wood there would be no paper and without the workbench there would be no desk on which to write, no chair to sit on while doing so, and no books that we can really touch and feel.

The Toolbox

This morning when I turned on my computer, I was informed that my tool-box had been updated! Yes, even our computers have toolboxes, which are of great value in getting the most out of your programs. I have never used all the tools in my computer's toolbox and as yet I have no idea what many can do. But I know that they can come in very useful if only I take the trouble to open my toolbox and examine what I've got and what each tool is capable of.

I think it must have been when I turned six that Mr. Smith, a good neighbor, made and gave me my first toolbox as a birthday present. As toolboxes go, it was rather small, but just right for me. Painted battleship grey, it had nine compartments in which to keep a handful of small tools, some screws and nails. A small clasp kept the lid shut and a metal handle enabled me to carry it. My father's toolbox, which now lies beneath my workbench, was a much larger and sturdier one with rope handles at each end. It has been around a long time and travelled the country with him as the family moved home. You don't get toolboxes like that unless you make them yourself. It was crude in comparison to the tool cabinets described in some of the books on the subject, but it served its purpose. Whether magnificent or lowly, toolboxes and cabinets provide safe storage for your tools, whether portable or fixed to the wall, and they make your tools easily accessible for when you need them.

•

That reminds me, John, about something Aneliese pointed out to me recently. When I go into the shop I first put on my apron, which contains all the little tools I need constantly, no matter what the job—pencils, square, small ruler, pliers, flashlight, box cutter, masking tape. Experience has taught me the list. I have one apron for general use and one for woodturning. They are my constant "tool boxes." It's as if I'm putting on my special costume for a special work.

•

Yes, indeed, Bill, I feel much the same. Incidentally, Stephen King, the well-known mystery, horror, and science fiction writer, in his book *On Writing: A Memoir of a Craft*, tells us about his Uncle Oren's toolbox filled to the brim with tools that he carried around from one job to the next. The box had three levels, and on each there was a layer of tools. On top were tools in daily use, but as Uncle Oren dug deeper he came across more specialized ones for tasks that required them. As every woodworker knows, there is always a tool for the job if only you keep looking for it. And, if you can't find it, you can always make a jig.

So too, King tells us, the writer's toolbox contains all the equipment that a writer needs—not just pen and paper, but vocabulary and grammar, the skills needed to unlock writer's block and develop creativity, and much more, all tools gathered during a lifetime of writing. Writers never stop discovering new ones and learning how to use them. That is why learning to write or any other craft takes a lifetime. We not only need a box full of tools—those we can acquire during a day's shopping in a hardware store—we need to learn how to use them, keep them sharp and clean, and know which tool is needed for what task. And we need to learn to use all the tools in our toolbox. You may be a master planer, but if you cannot saw or use a hammer correctly, that is not much good.

Anton has reminded me that in an attempt to get him to read more as a schoolboy, Isobel and I once bought him a book on tools for Christmas. It was, he recalls, big and heavy, but he would read it again and again, looking at the pictures and learning what each tool was used for. We still have that book on our shelves! Today, Anton is an ardent lover of tools, but he also knows that "you only own a tool when you truly know how to tune, maintain, and use it." I asked him to tell us more about his journey with tools, and this is what he wrote.

"I have always been fascinated by tools, tools of any sort. I like old tools, new tools, fancy tools and simple tools. Each one unique, yet fashioned for purpose. In fact, I am now beginning to make my own and have

 recently built my first wooden hand plane. Using them adds pleasure to the process. But whether hand tools or machines, tools bring vision to life, they are the means by which the image in our minds for a sculpture, a painting, or a piece of furniture becomes a reality. From the large table saw to the small marking knife, each one plays its part in making our vision come to life."

Anton continued, "When I started learning woodwork at high school I could not cut straight and had no idea how to use a chisel. For much of my early woodworking journey I assumed that I could not use hand tools and so became dependent on machines. But more and more I have come to realize that to do the kind of work I want to do I need to do more hand tool work. Making this transition and learning the techniques required to use each tool have become part of the fun of woodworking. This is no different than a musician learning what their instrument can do or a dancer perfecting a routine."

Anton, a fan of Sam Maloof's work, reminded me of the master craftsman's oft-quoted words: "There's a lot of work being done today that doesn't have any soul in it. The technique may be the utmost perfection, yet it is lifeless. It doesn't have a soul. I hope my furniture has a soul to it."[1] Anton then went on to say: "I believe that when we pick up our hand tools and hold the work in our hands we impart our own life and soul into the piece." Hand tools, he insists, make a "better connection between the hand, tool and wood, enable better control and accuracy, and bring more enjoyment, no different from a golfer getting pleasure from a perfect swing or a tennis player from the perfect serve." And maybe it also enables us to show more respect for the wood.

With this in mind, he quoted Maloof again: "The reverence that the object maker has for the materials, for the shape, and for the miracle of his skill transcends to God, the Master Craftsman, the Creator of all things, who uses us, our hands, as His tools to make these beautiful things."[2]

Bill, don't you think there is something Benedictine about all this?

~

The Work of Mediation

I would take it even further, John, and say that there is something sacramental about what's going on in these spaces with these instruments and materials. I was just talking with my third-generation woodworker friend, John Gernandt, whom you met on one of your visits. At one point in our conversation John, who is a top-notch furniture designer, interjected "You really love trees!" Not just how to design and craft an object from wood, but the living—and dying—tree itself. I think that for us, the tree in its natural state, whether stately or gnarled, twisted or massive, is a form of mediation between ourselves and the mysterious source of all being. I think that's what makes it somehow sacramental. That is surely one reason why it has had such a prominent place in the world's great religions. More personally, I have learned that not only are trees and woods mediators in themselves, but my relationship to them is a mediated one as well. While I can stroke the bark with my fingers, it is only through tools, almost always metal tools, that I can turn a tree into an object of utility that at the same time brings out the beauty inherent in the wood. Though the capacity to feel the wood is crucial, you can't do woodworking with your fingernails alone.

1. *Maloof on Maloof*, Smithsonian Institution online exhibition at americanart. si.edu/exhibitions/online/maloof/conclusion.

2. Maloof, *Sam Maloof: Woodworker*, 53.

The work often begins with the Stihl chainsaw that I have had for almost twenty-five years. Some of the trees I have cut down with it have been sawn into boards by friends who own portable sawmills. My older sister owns a barn nearby where I stack the boards to cure over a period of years. I also built a small wood kiln for the final drying of the wood, but that is rarely necessary. The chainsaw also enables me to cut shorter pieces of the logs for future woodturning projects. I spend a lot of time sorting, stacking, moving, and restacking wood. Woodworking requires the virtue of patience. Even the wood has to be patient, as it awaits its possible transformation.

What begins with the chainsaw moves on to a portable circular saw, band saw, and table saw, before moving to jointer and planer, chisel and hand plane, and, yes, lowly sandpaper. Whether a hand tool or a power tool, each tool reflects years, sometimes centuries, of development, with generations of woodworkers refining the instrument according to its purpose and the capacities of the human being operating it. One of my prized possessions is a set of Japanese chisels that I bought a few years ago on a trip to Japan. They should last several lifetimes with proper care and sharpening.

Now, to some degree we woodworkers can start making a fetish of our tools. Their purchase, maintenance, and appearance become ends in themselves. They become the idols of our woodcraft religion. We confuse means and ends. It's a spiritual problem, in a sense. In loving these beautiful tools we hold ourselves back from the test even of using them, of applying them to a precious piece of wood, possibly destroying it as well as enhancing it.

It seems to me that a lot of what we have been talking about is a matter of vocation, or calling. Matching the person to the tools, the wood, and the wider vision of its use is in itself a kind of vocational task. How we do it says something about our vocational sense as well as forming that sense in turn. Maybe this is another reason courses in woodworking are returning, not merely for retired people who are re-tooling their lives (I had to say it!), but for those just starting out in life. If you pushed me, I would suggest that woodworking, like other crafting with natural materials, should be a part of religious education and formation. This seems to be intrinsic to the life of many faith communities that seek to live apart from industrial civilization in pursuit of a spiritual ideal. The Shakers are probably our most influential historic example. One of the more treasured pieces of furniture in our home is a beautifully crafted walnut corner cupboard made in a Mennonite community in Virginia. Woodworking can be the substance not only of personal vocation but of communal vocations as well.

I am reminded here of my friend and former colleague John Freeman, who told me how he gained a whole new sense of competency in his life through learning the craft of woodturning. He got to know an old craftsman in the hills near his home in upstate South Carolina who used only a set of scrapers he fashioned from old files to turn out attractive bowls with his Sears lathe. John thought, "Well, if he can do that, maybe I might be able to turn something out." And indeed, since then he has been turning all sorts of things, and to his amazement, selling them in local fairs. But what was important to him was how a few simple tools, some wood, and a lathe were mediators of transformation in his life. My son Eric has likewise told me that when he began to teach woodworking skills to girls in his theater class, they pitched in with enthusiasm and gained a whole new sense of self-confidence. It's a great liberation to move from being cogs in a wheel to actually making the cogs and a lot of other things!

Working with wood served as a form of mediation and transformation for me as well. As I was working on the round communion table for Andover Newton Theological School, which I'll talk about in a minute, a doctoral student of mine with a background in psychotherapy observed that it was for me a "transitional object." The phrase, coined by the psychologist Donald Winnicott, usually refers to an object like a stuffed toy that enables an infant to move from attachment to his or her mother to a wider world of supportive objects. In my case, the emerging table was a bridge from the academic life I had led since adulthood into a different configuration of support and confirmation.

For some time my work in academic life and administration had felt increasingly narrow and unrewarding, not so much in public confirmation as in interior satisfaction. I thought that a move to a new institution would answer this need, but it gradually became apparent that it could not. One sleepless night, as I was in my late fifties, I had a vivid sense of a voice, as if from some Jungian persona, saying to me, "It is enough. It is time to move on to something different." Somehow, I knew that this involved some kind of work with my hands. Looking back on it, I think I had been preparing for this unconsciously, not only in gradually acquiring tools for my shop in North Carolina, but also through my collaboration with Sylvia, who had led me into her world of artistic production in textiles, mosaics, and found materials.

As you mentioned earlier, there was also a financial base to this transition. I would soon be able to draw from pension funds that my sponsoring institutions had contributed to over the years. Along with Social Security and a later inheritance, I was able to turn to work that the industrial economy has long ago pushed to the extreme margins of society. Only a very few people can make a living from the kind of craft in wood and words that was calling me into a new way of living. I was being led into the kind of work celebrated by the arts and crafts movements in England and America at the end of the nineteenth century. Here in North Carolina, where it made a significant mark on the cultural landscape, I would myself enter into some strands of this movement to recover the craft and care of material artisanry. However, the oppressive economic shadow that prevents so many talented people from walking this path is often on my mind. I guess, John, that that is one reason why we are writing this book. We would like to help retrieve the spirit of this craft for others and not just ourselves, regardless of anyone's economic niche.

Soon after announcing that I would retire ("early," they said; "just in time," said I) from my position, I set about building the round communion table that would be my parting gift to Andover Newton Theological School. In struggling with its design, with the acquisition of wood from our local forests, and then turning to the joinery, the inlay, and the finishing, I began the process of moving into a greater interiority of purpose, a harmony with natural materials and processes, and a more harmonious wedding of mind and body that had eluded me throughout my academic career. The experience with the wounded strength of our tulip tree had foreshadowed this recovery of my body and my struggle for a greater harmony in my life, not only within my body-soul but also within the larger creation.

The table became a means of transition from the near-exclusive focus on ideas and conceptualization to a dialogue between vision and natural materials. It was a material way to move from the values of intellectual life about ultimate order and purpose to a fuller bodily engagement with one of the most precious materials sustaining our life. In a sense, it was a medium of personal conversion. I would guess, though I haven't done much research on this matter, that "transitional objects" play a bigger role in our life journey than we realize. Perhaps for some people this object may be a person—a love affair, a person in need—for others, perhaps a musical instrument, a house, or a pet. For me, it was a communion table. This became my transitional object, emerging at the confluence of my theological development and my need to marry hand and mind in a more harmonious way.

Building with Wood

Bill's Round Table

For many years my theological interests had revolved around the task of moving from a monarchical and patriarchal model for faith and religious language to one that reflects the values of democratic, constitutional republics. In short, I was working on my own version of the larger social change from hierarchical to circular processes of governance. In 1991 and 1992, I had done research on the rise of the "roundtable" experience in the early stages of German reunification after the fall of the Berlin Wall. I had written of these roundtables as little nuclei of the public order for which people were yearning.

I subsequently wrote a small book detailing the way worship forms could integrate the circle experience of reconciliation and conflict transformation into the very core of worship. In this view, worship is a rehearsal of the reconciled relations of God's new creation yet to come. So, from the intellectual side, I was ready to make this a practical reality. With the maturation of these ideas, my inner being spoke its readiness to address this task more physically. The design began to emerge in my mind. The table that would reflect this understanding of worship as a rehearsal of reconciliation would be a double gate-leg table. The drop-leaves supported by the gate-legs would contain inlays of symbols of baptism and communion—dove, seashell, Trinity, grapes, wheat.

It was natural for me to turn to the woods around me for materials. At first, with the aid of Eric and a local friend (my insurance agent Don Overbay, in fact) I sliced boards from a large cherry log from my property to make the legs, but they would require too much time to cure, so Don ended up offering me some cherry large enough to make the legs. The rest of the wood—cherry for the pedestal and hard maple for the top—I bought at

Gennett Lumber, one of the region's oldest hardwood lumberyards, whose history stretches back to the earliest days of scientific forestry here in these mountains.

My failure to use the cherry from my own land was due to the fact that hardwoods need to cure in the air for one year for each inch of thickness. Kiln drying reduces that time to a few weeks, but it usually robs the wood of some of its beauty. At the very outset, my desire to move quickly from plan to reality encountered the slow time of natural processes. I learned that the first virtue of woodworking is patience. It is built into the very nature of the wood itself. I would have to await the wood's time as it gave up its water to the air, moving from a moisture content of 30 percent to only 6 or 7 percent. I would have to be patient as it settled its fibers to lie flat for my plane. I would have to take the time to check design against measurements, grain, and figure to reduce splitting, checking, and chipping at the ends. Method and patience would join to slow me down, focus my mind and hands, and eliminate the multi-tasking and distractions that had shaped my life for decades. Just as I had had to labor over footnotes and citations, so now I labored over shaping wood to fit its fellow members, align with my design, yield its beauty to the eye and hand. But I still had much to learn.

In making the table I had set out on a different way of understanding how we communicate values and perspectives that change our lives. The table would not seek to shape people's lives through the process of seeing and hearing words. "Hearing the Word"—that was the way of my Protestant ancestors. In the words of a German book I had read years ago, I was raised more as an "ear-man" (*Ohrenmensch*) than the "eye-man" (*Augenmensch*) of Catholic sensibilities. The *Augenmensch* found revelation not by hearing words but by seeing the colors, visions, architecture, and forms of sculptures, furniture, and figures brought together in the rituals of worship. And even more, like any piece of furniture, the table organized the relationships among people, shaping their movements in a space. It shaped action in a way different from the commands contained in words. The table emphasizes the way we are "*Kinetischmensch*"—kinetic humans— who learn and communicate through the way we move our bodies. In short, it is a world of dance, of choreography. I was not only building a table for worship, I was entering into a new understanding about how deeper realities are mediated, indeed, revealed, to us.

Unlike the inherent individualism of the Protestant focus on reading the Word, the table invites people into a communal action of eating, drinking, and conversation. It was inherently social, if not necessarily truly public. I had been prepared for this by many years of teaching in a Catholic seminary and immersing myself in its liturgy during that wonderful time of ecumenical engagement after Vatican II. Now it was flowing to my hands and my connection to the forests and people of these mountains.

At this point I had to refine my drawings of the table to arrive at exact measurements for each piece. Now here is where the details really matter! It's actually taken me years to really respect the importance of the construction drawing. There is an inevitable math behind the world's design. It's at this point that I start muttering about our failure to adopt a metric system in this country. Sometimes I feel like an author writing on papyrus.

•

Bill, "I can feel your pain," as one of your Presidents said. When I was doing woodwork in junior school all our measurements were in imperial or standard inches and feet. South Africa only switched to metric in 1961. All of a sudden we had to work in millimeters, centimeters, and meters, just as our currency switched from pounds and shillings to rands and cents. The transition wasn't as difficult as we had thought and nobody I know has ever regretted the change. I know something about the difficulties involved in making such a change in the US, but I do think it is a great pity that it never happened when the chance came. Oh, well, let me not get embroiled in that controversy, though I know you are on my side! Fortunately we can now get tape measures that are in both standard and metric, so that helps when we are working together. I must also say that I am the equivalent of ambidextrous when it comes to using both systems in any case, and often think in terms of inches and feet, as well as miles. This is not true of my children, and certainly not of my grandchildren. But you and I have had our moments working together when mistakes crept in because of our two systems.

Do you remember the rosewood entrance hall table I made, the one with the turned legs, and how you arrived to give a hand just when I was fitting the drawers? I have never quite worked out why we did not get the left hand one to fit properly (though only you and I know that—and God), but when I think about it, I wonder whether the problem was that we were measuring differently! I am not sure, mind you, and since the drawer works reasonably well I will let the matter rest. Of course, you may have a different reason for the mistake. But I know that ever since then we have been extra careful when working together. The truth is, and many who obtain tools across borders don't always get this, you can't just buy plug cutters and router bits in the US or the UK and expect them to fit in Europe or South Africa. A 1/4" router bit simply does not fit into an 8mm router, nor does a 1/2" plug cutter cut plugs that will fit a 10 mm hole! The difference may appear slight, but it is more than enough to create problems. I have had router bits simply fall out in the middle of a job, making a mess of a table edge in doing so, because of this.

While on measuring, let me repeat here what I am sure everybody who is anybody in the woodworking business knows, but it is still the best advice ever given: "Measure twice, cut once." I taught this adage to an assistant, Darrington Nceka, I had early on at Volmoed and he soon learnt its importance. But on one occasion when I made a total mess up cutting wood for one of our projects on the bandsaw, he muttered under his breath: "You seem to have cut seven times and measured only once!" Darrington was right. I will always remember him, not only for that reason, but because he had a fetish for tidying up at the end of the sessions so thoroughly that I sometimes had difficulty in finding my tools. So my habit now is that when Serghay and I end a day's work, everything gets back to where it should be in one of my tool cabinets, and I make sure he knows where everything belongs. A great time and frustration saver.

Incidentally, Serghay and I don't have a problem with metric, but sometimes we do with language. He is Afrikaans speaking and while I am reasonably fluent in it, and he reasonably fluent in English, now and again technical terms elude us. So we have learnt to make sure we are understanding each other to prevent mishaps. Say it twice or thrice if need be, and you might avoid cutting your fingers! I never thought that multi-culturalism would be an issue in the workshop, but it is. Even communication between you and me sometimes flounders when you insist on speaking improper English!

•

And Southern at that, John! But your recall of communication in the shop amplifies my awareness of our need for mediators, which is a nice way to return to my story of the round table—my symbol of mediation and reconciliation. After gathering the cherry and maple, and ordering some thin wood for the inlays (holly from Georgia, purpleheart from Central America, walnut from regional forests), I set about planing it to proper thickness before cutting it to size. So much of woodworking, like sculpture, is a process of elimination, of cutting away. Anything of beauty, depth, and staying power arises out of purging. Whether it is the refiner's fire of biblical visions, the ascetic practices of fasting or exile, the self-emptying of genuine love—it is all a cutting away of what is not needed. Working with wood has a way of guiding you to "the one thing most needful." The shavings and sawdust would go into the compost (except the walnut, which is toxic!) or into my wood stove in the winter. It would all be useful. But the table would arise from the cutting away. My hands and their tools were doing what religious traditions had long proclaimed.

With the wood prepared, I had to fashion tenons and the mortises to receive them at just the right places. In marking out the placements I had to keep moving my mind back and forth between the parts and the whole. How does the entire table fit together and what does this imply for this particular part? Which will be the facing surface? Which will be inside? As I struggled with this task of joinery, I realized how important this capacity to think constantly about part to whole extends to all of life.

One of the requirements of cabinetry, with all its parts, is that you have to label everything. You can even find these marks hidden deep inside old cabinets as well as new ones such as my own. Arrows point up, down, and out. Letters and numbers identify each piece—its overall dimensions, its tenons or mortises, its dado grooves or mating surfaces. It's way more complicated than Adam's task in the Garden. Not just cherry this and walnut that, but Part A4, this end up, this side out, mortise here, glue face there. I can't count how many times a failure to do this completely and thoroughly has gotten me in trouble.

All this has reminded me that our failure to think relationally lies beneath our ecological crisis and our inability to think of our place within a more universal system. It accompanies our persistence, especially in my American culture, of thinking about rights (the part) more than responsibilities (my relation to the whole). Joinery, or cabinetry, as others have pointed out, fosters a cooperative, communal, and collaborative sense of being part of a whole, one member in an ensemble. It's a strain of thought and values that went through John Ruskin, William Morris, and the Arts and Crafts movement in the nineteenth century. Working on the table was a way of re-awakening this connection of artisanry, communalism, and a table-centered Christianity.

A failure to think in this relational way consistently led me to make mistakes. The mortises were too wide or in the wrong place. In one case it simply meant that the best side of the leg would face in rather than out. I accepted this. In other cases, it meant I had to patch in some shims to give the tenons a tight fit.

Because of the very nature of a tree, lumber usually comes in straight boards of varying lengths, width, and thickness. This is what makes it "lumber" rather than "wood." And indeed, much of the furniture fashioned from it has straight lines and right angles. Keeping things aligned on these axes is a constant preoccupation as I move around with square, straight-edge, and calipers.

However, roundness is also a quality of being a tree. Unfortunately the roundness is weak because of the way grain works. Wood is essentially a bundle of straws bound together. It splits along the straws and holds firm against forces that seek to break the straws. Whether we're turning wood on the lathe along the line of these straws or against them, we always have to keep in mind this fundamental fact. So now, I hope this gives the old phrase "grasping at straws" a new meaning, for that's what I'm doing all the time when I'm working with wood!

To make a round table, I would have to drill a pivot screw at its center and anchor my router a couple of feet out from it on a plexiglass arm. Then, with a roundover bit, I would walk around the table, in this case some sixty inches across, deepening the bit a little with each pass. How strange, that I was circumambulating the table in the way monks and priests walk around an altar. Because of the way the bit addresses the grain, I had to walk in a counter-clockwise direction in order to minimize tear-out and produce an even edge—a monk in reverse. (Although I've noticed that pilgrims in Mecca walk counter-clockwise around the Kaaba.) In any case, I was walking into the dance the wood required to become the round table of communion I intended.

Of course, there are always mistakes. As my woodworking friend Ed Davis, says, "A mistake is when the piece leaves the shop. Otherwise, it's a creative design feature." But fixing an error in wood is not a simple matter of erasure or deletion, as it had been in my writing. An error in wood leads either to starting over completely or to figuring out an adaptive repair. Whenever possible, I choose the latter. With the mortise it is easy. Shim it in. As John Gernandt has said to me, "Even God doesn't see the inside of a mortise." Well, maybe. But I did. I live with it as a repair. And indeed, the practice of repair has gained increasing salience in my life. This is what the wood was working into my muscles and bones.

I had just spent ten years writing and researching about reconciliation dynamics in India, Germany, America, and South Africa. Indeed, a common interest in this is what originally drew us into correspondence, as I recall. I had been thinking about reconciliation and forgiveness from the perspective of restorative justice. I had been arguing that restoration and repair must replace our fixation on retribution and punishment. Understanding justice as restorative rather than retributive lies at the heart of our efforts to reform the criminal justice system, not to mention addressing the damage of climate change and warfare.

Now the act of woodcraft was telling me the same thing, working it into my hands and imagination. Woodworking is always a matter of treating the wood justly, of repairing mistakes and accidental injuries. Even when complete repair is not possible, mistakes can be incorporated to enhance the authenticity and integrity of the piece itself. It is a work that humbles us and shapes our imagination of how to deal with the evils that shadow our designs of beauty and our intentions of utility.

Even these designs and intentions have their limits. However, every woodworker knows that the wood establishes its own integrity over against our intentions, whether through the course of its grain, the presence of a knot or burl, or internal tensions built up during its growth and struggle with its circumstances. It is not simply a matter of imposing our will on the wood, but of a kind of dialogue with it that enables it to yield its inner beauty and strength as well as its peculiarities and "imperfections." Here, the wood reveals the stress of a crotch between branches. There it evidences the socket where a branch had formed. At every point its grain reveals dry years and wet, hospitable warmth and searing cold. The wood reveals its history and the forces that have shaped its life.

For me, as for most of us, I assume, the image of the craftsman has often been our lens for understanding God. Whether as potter or master architect, God is seen as one who imposes his (the tradition always says "his") will on us, the clay, the wood, the raw inert material. But this leaves out the dialogical relation of worker and wood. Even to the degree I might understand myself as wood, as a tree if you will, there is a realm of free engagement, out of which we can speak not only of a God of love but of love and justice as the highest blessedness to which creatures can aspire. We are not simply living out a Divine Plan but participating, with our own integrity, in a larger drama out of which can emerge beauty and serviceability.

~

Finding the Grain

Bill, what you say about respecting the integrity of the wood we work with resonates with me. I recall that one of my Australian friends, Mary Williams, once told me that some of my weekly chapel meditations at Volmoed work on her "imagination and soul a bit like a craftsman's lathe—finding the grain, then going with it to discover its sometimes surprising innate loveliness." This, she concluded, "takes a lifetime, too!" Yes, indeed, finding the grain and in doing so being surprised by its "innate loveliness" is one of the joys of woodturning. An idea, sometimes clear in the mind and carefully calculated, but often not, takes shape as the chips fly. And as the sawdust settles or is sucked away, a chunk of wood becomes an object of beauty.

You can imagine my excitement, then, as a bowl begins to take shape on my lathe, dictating its future form as much as I do, as though I am all the time consulting with the wood, molding it like clay on a wheel according to its own inbred character. This is the fun, joy, and wonder of turning. I also think this is what education and Christian formation is about: allowing the uniqueness of each person to be brought to the surface, enabling the inside core, or soul, to reveal itself in its own way and time, until the amazing grain that lies within is seen in all its beauty and radiance. Turning bowls is a parable of discerning and enabling the growth of embodied soul.

For those who are listening in to our conversation, maybe I should say a word or two here, Bill, about how we understand the word "soul." After all, we have highlighted it in the title of our book. But the word is a slippery one, which is why many theologians speak today more about the inner "self," or the "person" we really are. Helpful as those expressions are, they lack the weight of tradition, they also need clarification, and they are often more psychological in substance than theological. I think the clue, at least to the biblical notion of the soul, lies in its conjunction with "embodied." Contrary to the widely held view that the soul is an immortal, divine, and discrete essence in each individual, an inner "little being" as some have stereotyped it, we ought to understand it in complex, dynamic, and relational terms that express embodied human uniqueness. As human beings, we are constantly changing psycho-somatic wholes in relation to God and the world. Deeply embedded in our prehistoric past, yet expanding into the future, we "embodied souls" are always in a process of becoming, whether through physical growth and decay, or through intentional and self-conscious development towards a personal and spiritual maturity that is sometimes described as the "journey of the soul" or a journey into wholeness. I like John Polkinghorne's description of the soul as "the almost infinitely complex, dynamic, information-bearing pattern in which the matter of our bodies at any one time is organized."[3]

This reminds me of an old woman I met one day driving home from Cape Town to Volmoed. She was standing by the roadside in the rain. Her outward appearance reminded me of the rough gnarled bark on the olive wood sitting back home on my lathe. I stopped my bakkie and offered her a ride to wherever she was going. After driving for twenty miles and

3. Polkinghorne, "Eschatological Credibility," 51.

conversing about her family, I discovered something beautiful hidden deep within. When I eventually said farewell, I pondered on the fact that so often we judge others by appearance. We see an old lady standing by the roadside looking the worse for wear, not a person, an "embodied soul" with a life story to share, with similar experiences of sadness and sorrow to our own. Like the grain beneath the bark of an old tree, there was a "surprising innate loveliness" I would never have discovered had she remained another one of those anonymous people waiting and waiting on the roadside for someone to stop, another chunk of wood crying out to be turned in order to reveal its innate beauty. She would have remained, for me, a body without soul.

Such "embodied" encounters also help us recover our own souls. That is why we need to see people as we see ourselves, not as some category of unfortunates, but a widow who has lost a son, a granny who treasures her five remaining children and their children, a person with a life-long story to share, a hidden beauty beneath the surface, a lovely grain underneath the bark that has grown up around her to protect what lies underneath. For that is what bark does—it keeps the beauty safe rather than displaying it as a thin veneer that cannot take too much wear and tear.

This reminds me that while we do not have portraits of Jesus of Nazareth, we do have stories about what he did and said. It is not Jesus' appearance that draws us to him. What attracts us is something that speaks to the soul. It is all about the way he treated people, especially those despised and shunned by the religious and social leaders of the day. His beauty was an innate loveliness that enabled him to see that which lay beneath the surface in others, recognizing them as human beings made in the image of God. Maybe he learned this when he was working on a foot-peddled lathe in his father's workshop, marveling at the lovely grain that emerged once you had got beneath the rough bark. I like to think so. Maybe that is why I have also come to think that trees have souls, that is, a hidden identity that shapes their character as we encounter them, just as it shaped the widow I met along the road.

This thought was prompted by a beautiful coffee-table book Anton gave me for Christmas in 2013 entitled *The Soul of a Tree* by George Nakashima. Nakashima was the foremost woodworker and cabinet-maker in North America in the twentieth century. A Japanese American by birth, he studied architecture in Japan and Paris, and then followed his passion in designing and building beautiful furniture. In *The Soul of a Tree,* he tells his life's story. He also describes his way of making furniture—from the selection of the wood through to the finishing touches.

There is so much in the book that I found inspiring as well as challenging as a woodworker, but I also found spiritual insight and wisdom in its pages. Nakashima had a deep love and respect for trees. He often walked in the forests near where he lived on the East Coast of the United States, and had an intimate knowledge of trees from all parts of the world. He saw beyond their outward appearance to their inner beauty, and this enabled him to select the wood he needed in order to make beautiful furniture. His furniture was not ostentatious as though he was in competition with the wood, trying to make it more beautiful. His aim was to allow the inner beauty of the tree to reveal itself in what he made. For me, the most memorable comment Nakashima made was that a tree can have two lives. First, as a tree growing to maturity and then, at the right time and not before, when it is harvested and transformed into something beautiful at the hands of a craftsman. In his own words: "There is a drama in the opening of a log—to uncover for the first time the beauty . . . of a tree hidden for centuries, waiting to be given this second life."[4]

The genius of a master craftsman like Nakashima is that he can give new birth to a tree. Through his skills, the beauty locked in a tree is brought to life again as a table, or chair, or cabinet to bring joy to many. I am in a very junior league compared to the likes of Nakashima, but I am also excited when, on working with wood, I discover a beautiful grain that I had not expected to find beneath the bark. This does not happen when I buy wood already planed and cut at Penny Pinchers. It might be fine pine or meranti for making something functional—an artist's easel, a work table or what have you. But when I obtain some mahogany or red oak, some camphor or olive, some walnut or kiaat that is still rough, and maybe still enclosed in bark, and begin to work with it on the lathe, or open it up with the saw and plane, I can't wait to discover the secrets beneath the surface, its inner character that will, in many ways, determine what I make. It is this hidden secret or soul that has developed over years, even centuries, which is the source of its nurture and growth, and evolving beauty. Without this inner life, the heartwood enclosed by sapwood, the tree would die. It might appear simple in structure and plain in color, as in the maple tree or ash, or it might be complex and exotic, as in wild olive or kiaat, but it is beautiful whichever way you look at it. I guess this is why many of us are attracted to icons of Jesus, for they penetrate beneath the surface to reveal the beauty of the Christ of faith.

I recently met a woodcarver from Zimbabwe, Boniface Chikwenhere, whose stunning driftwood creations of birds and animals caught my eye at the local farmers' market one Saturday morning. Boniface sources his wood in many places, even remote dried up riverbeds or freshly exposed mountain cliffs, but then a miracle occurs as his hands get to work. "How

---

4. Nakashima, *The Soul of a Tree*, 93.

do you know what you will carve when you find a likely piece of wood?" I asked him. "I don't," he replied, "I let the wood tell me."

My sculptor friend, Bill Davis, saw the beauty of the crucified and risen Christ in a fallen branch of a camphor tree here on Volmoed. With skill and dexterity he brought that image to life, and it now hangs behind the altar in the sanctuary. It was carved out of several pieces of branches that had broken off a large camphor tree during a wintry storm one night at Volmoed. Bill immediately saw the potential in the branch not just for carving the figure of Christ but also for making a theological statement. He later wrote:

"When I took the almost completed figure to the sanctuary to check if the size was correct, and to see how I should attach the arms and hands, it struck all of us who were there that the incomplete figure, without arms and hands, had become a powerful reminder of Christ's suffering and relates directly to the Volmoed theme: 'bringing wholeness to broken people.' Through the figure leaning slightly forward we experience his identifying with each person's pain and brokenness and the significance of his offer of himself to set us free. The rough surface is intentional to intensify the brokenness and suffering depicted in the Christ figure. The lack of arms, as if blasted off, suggests that all the violent and terrorist deeds of our present time hurt our Lord and that he physically feels all the pain. The arm stumps are the natural branches of the actual tree. A cross was not necessary as the figure depicts the risen Christ."

You can only do what a tree or wood allows you to do, but often it evokes more than at first seems possible. If you let your imagination loose, you can discern something that the wood is inviting you to do, something more profound or beautiful than you first thought. Every icon or great painting of Jesus, like Bill Davis' sculpture, is different from the next. But each brings to the surface something of the mystery of the face of God or the human soul, whether we happen to be an old gnarled oak, a hardy acacia, apple tree, or a piece of driftwood on the seashore. I guess it is learning to know something the wood already knows! Anton tells me that hand tools give us this "feedback about the wood. They free up the creative process and the ability to design work that is more organic." Bill Davis' work as a carver demonstrates that this is so.

~

Knowing the Wood

Yes, indeed! Bill Davis' sculpture is one of the most vivid works of wood in my memory. You're lucky to have that wonderful piece in your chapel at Volmoed. It reminds me that the kind of knowing that wood teaches us goes beyond our powers of vision and cognition. It involves all our senses. As I moved into the stages of sanding my first round table, I realized increasingly how important touch is to this work. It is not a faculty I had used in my academic work. Touch reveals far more than the eye can see, as every woodworker knows. When I move to a finer grit of sandpaper, I can see the scratches left by the coarser grit, but it is my hands that confirm the overall impact of the surface and the piece. It is their hands that people will want to rub over the surface to feel its smoothness, the great or small resistance of this particular wood. We know the wood by touching it. Maybe this is why lovers long to touch each other in order to fully know and be known. Maybe this is why we long for more than a merely ethereal God. We long for a body to touch, for soul is always embodied.

But the woodworking was awakening more than simply an awareness of knowledge through touch. It was also giving new meaning to "practical knowledge." A lot of religious and spiritual talk is abstract and theoretical, or couched in biblical or theological language remote from our experience. It is a speculative or theoretical way of knowing. More recently, theologians have tried to talk about practical knowledge as important to religious life. Certainly, that would seem to be important to the average person seeking a deeper faith. But even with "practical theology," I have felt it had an abstract character, a talking *about* practices. Or it was simply another way of talking about virtue, values, norms, and rights. But what about the actual practice of engaging materials in a transformative way, both for the material and for the crafter?

•

If I may interrupt, I like what you say about practical knowledge, Bill. I am not sure how useful impractical knowledge can be—sounds like an oxymoron! But a great deal of so-called knowledge with which we are both familiar from our years in the academy could do with some debunking and demythologizing, I think! Practical knowledge, however, is not just knowledge that helps us do "practical things" like woodworking, it is actually wisdom, that is, a knowledge that helps us think clearly and logically, imagine creatively as we seek to solve a problem, to challenge humbug, and the skill to transfer thoughts into deeds.

•

Yes, the skills for transformation. In my woodwork I was training and re-training certain muscles, some of them long dormant, disciplining my hands (at first I wrote "discipling"!) as mediators between tool and mind, wood and intention. It became a process of focusing the self in a way that renewed a sense of wholeness and integrity. It was not only a knowing of the woods and their various particularities, but of myself as a creative agent. I was tired at the end of the day but not exhausted. The wood was starting to heal and reintegrate me.

There is one thing that would sometimes enter my efforts to fall asleep or wake up. I found myself rehearsing the next day's engagements. How would I set up a jig for the mortises? What would be the sequence for shaping some pieces? Would I mortise them first and then introduce a curve in the leg? I began to feel like an actor in a play I was rehearsing. The crafting of materials was as much a dramatic performance as a public theater. In the years leading up to the table, I had come to the conclusion that our worship should be seen as a kind of rehearsal of God's emerging republic of peace. The actual performance with the wood might reveal mistakes to be repaired, but rehearsal might obviate some, might school me for a more effective performance. All this rehearsing was especially important as I approached the inlays.

People often ask me how I do these inlays, as if it were a magical or highly esoteric practice. But it isn't. First, I begin to imagine the design, then I select the woods whose figure, grain, and color best contribute to the overall symbolism of the inlay. Usually I order small boards cut to 1/8" thickness or I plane them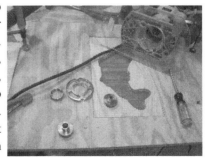

myself. I then make templates from plywood with saws and drills. And finally, I attach various diameter bushings around the base of my router— narrower ones to cut out the inlay, wider ones to cut the mortise in the table that receives them. Well, OK, it is complicated, but not magical. The problem is that you simply can't make a mistake cutting the mortise. No repair will "make it right." You can cut a new inlay piece, but a mortise mistake effectively destroys the tabletop's beauty. That's why the rehearsing is so important. What direction to move the router in order to avoid tearing the grain? What is the best way to support the router as it moves? When is the depth of the mortise just right? All of this is rehearsed until I feel comfortable entering the task. Preparing a lecture or sermon was easier than this.

•

Bill, I don't know what it says about my sermons, but I keep all inlays as simple as possible. I don't use a router to cut the mortise, as I prefer to use drilling and razor sharp chisels. Forstner bits are excellent for getting the depth precise and flat, and the chisels cut nice clean outlines. I use my carving tools for those sections which are not straight. I cut the mortises first and then make the tenons either on my bandsaw or on my fret saw, shaping them until they fit snugly and are about 1/8" proud. Paring with a chisel and some sanding completes the task. But much also depends on the wood I use—some sorts just don't do inlays!

•

There are indeed more ways than one to cut an inlay, John! I guess habit dictates a great deal. And for me it is easier to do curves and circles this way. Maybe there is a lesson in practical knowledge here as well. The inlays

 for my first round table were actually of two kinds. The inlays on the drop-leaves, I decided, would be of walnut and holly. The inlay in the center would be a glass tile mosaic created by Sylvia, who had become expert in this medium. Under her tutelage since then I have become more proficient with these mosaic inlays. But then I had to address the question of how the wood's expansion and

contraction through the seasons would affect the inlays. The grain of the wood inlays must parallel that of the table. You can depart from this rule only to a small extent before the inlay is popped from the mortise in the course of a year. How great an extent is something I learned to my embarrassment a few years later, but that's a different story! I was counting on the slight coefficient of expansion in the grout between the tile pieces to allow for wood movement in the center. I even have a chart listing the "C. O. E" of the major lumber woods to help me gauge this.

All of this is to say that wood is not dead. It keeps breathing with the lungs of the world. It is part of the movement of the earth as it wobbles round the sun. It participates in the wind and climate as well as the temperature around it. Indeed, it exemplifies the fact that the world around us is not "dead" or "inanimate," but part of a common metabolism—the breathing of the world. And, indeed, without the tree's gift of oxygen we would not be breathing at all. We are derivative of the trees. We are in a dance with them. To break out of the dance is to lose our life. Our task is to learn the dance and to observe its steps, to live in the embrace as a breathing among breaths.

With the inlays done, I turned to the finish. Because the table would face years of institutional use, I decided not to use a hand-rubbed finish for the pedestal, but to put on several coats of polyurethane. To preserve the clarity of the top I used a clear acrylic. For most pieces, I prefer hand-rubbed finishes, which are more laborious. Each coat is rubbed three times, with a total of four or five coats before I reach the luster that I like. The wood is rubbed over and over like some beloved horse, bonding not only the finish but the finisher to the object of her or his ministrations. But here practicality took precedence over beauty. As I laid down the coats of finish with a brush, with light sanding in between, I could reflect back on the tension and intertwining of the life of action, which I had surveyed through the concepts of ethics, and artisanry, with its effort to shape a "material" world according to an ideal of beauty.

Hannah Arendt, a philosopher who has greatly affected my own thought, wrote in *The Human Condition* of the difference between action, work, and labor. Each human activity gives rise to its own thought processes and value systems. The transitional work of the table posed a question about my own identity, for I had spent much of my life focused on the world of action, but as an ethicist I had striven to make it conform to the artisan-like world of work. That is, I had approached action in terms of conformity to a plan, an ideal, a vision of harmony and proportion. In short, I had approached it as an artist devoted to beauty rather than as a politician devoted to glorious fame and storied memory. And "politician," as I had discovered, was not in my DNA. At most I was a skillful diplomat, a role that had lost its savor in my later years. So, free in retirement from the routines of labor, I was going through a passage of identity. The wood was introducing me to a self that lay behind the work of my public career. The wood was teaching me about myself and my inner core, what you have called my "soul."

This revelation has taken a long time to seep into my self-understanding. It has gradually effected a shift in my spirit and in the way I approach the world and other people. Much of this transition hinges around the values of publicity and privacy. Perhaps it was my roots in Washington, DC, but public life has always been a primary value for me. Indeed, much of my career has been an advancement of civic republican symbols and values as crucial to our understanding of theological understandings of sin, salvation, and grace. The world of patriarchal monarchy, which had captured Christian symbolism and spirituality for most of its history, had to be refurbished to express the perfect "publicity" of God's Republic. Indeed, I came to speak of this new order as a "republic" rather than use the traditional term "kingdom of God."

However, this publicity, this fullness of life, I can now see, can take two forms. In its classical form, "publicity" would be a personal performance of an individual in the drama of life before others. However, in the artisan world, the focus is not on the self but on the work that is presented to the world. The artist, working largely in private, fashions this object that speaks its own beauty and service in the world, shaping public space and the way people interact with each other. It is not about the artist, though our celebrity-ridden world loves to celebrate them, but about the work itself.

This humility of the artisan does not, therefore, mean a withdrawal from public life, but a different approach to it, one that prizes the work rather than the worker. The humility of the artisan is a humility not only before the materials of her or his craft, but also before the source (or should I write Source?) of creativity that enables the crafter to bring forth useful beauty in the object. It is not self-abasement but material devotion. St. Augustine had taught that the essence of religion was "humility, humility, humility." I had rejected that formulation because it was cast in the public-denying stance of his ascetic dualism between "this world" and the "next." Now I could better understand how the humility of working with wood arises in a constructive engagement with material reality, with the living creation, no less a gift of God than the coming new creation of biblical prophecy.

As important as this kind of work is, the artisan is always under threat, both from the factory organization of work under industrial capitalism and also from the obsession with fame and celebrity that drives the media-based economy. Crafters of wood are often looked down on socially as well as economically. Here in the mountains of the Blue Ridge and the Smokies, I live among some of the finest artisans in the world, along with some writers who can spin a yarn and ignite the soul. Almost all of them, however, are economically marginal, dependent on the wealthy few. The artisan's work of creating beauty and utility from natural materials is, it seems to me, intrinsic to what it is to be human, but observers since Adam Smith and Karl Marx have long lamented its virtual disappearance from ordinary economic life. But the resurgence of craft work, some of it exquisite, in the lives of the retired and the marginally employed (and even the imprisoned!) bespeaks the core human values of care, craft, beauty, and engagement with the natural world—and with others.

There's a lot of solitary work in this craft, but woodworking is not only the solitary engagement of crafter, tool, and wood. It is also a communal activity. As I work alone in my shop, planing, sanding, fitting, and finishing the woods of these mountains, I am continually reminded of the community in which I work and on which I depend for my materials, assistance, and guidance. We don't clear-cut in these mountains. Foresters and sawyers select individual hardwoods for harvesting. Much of my lumber comes from trees on or near my own land. The rest comes from people in hardwood lumberyards who know their woods. And then there are my woodworker friends, like Ed and John, who let me use one or another of their specialized machines, offer me tips, and give me encouragement, while I share in the delight of a pleasing piece from their own hands.

At the end of that summer, arising out of this community of trees and people, the table was finally complete. It would move from a community of artificers to a community of worshippers. But there had been a change in my own spirit and values, just as I hoped the table would work a change in spirit and value in those who gathered around it. It was through my hands but now it was out of my hands.

> Good stock
> cut straight
> with figure difficult,
> close grain complex,
> resistant to the metal blade,
> Yields up a plane, a curve,
> > negotiates with hands that bring it docile to a vision,
> > takes up a life beyond its death
> > assumes a proud utility
> > with beauty pulsing in its heart.
> The tools are laid aside,
> > their work fulfilled.
> The wood now burnished
> > with the craftsman's soul
> > shines forth in praise and gratitude.

~

John's Octagonal Table

Thank you, Bill, for baring your soul in your struggle through difficult times, and how this became embodied in your craft and especially your round communion table. My experience has been different, not least because I have not had to journey through the same crises as you. For me, the academic life is still a meaningful vocation, that is why in retirement I have continued to be engaged in the academy—mentoring, researching and writing. And, I guess, public engagement is part of who I am! But, like you, woodworking has often been a solace for the soul, not least during the weeks that followed Steve's death. That terrible and tragic happening coincided with my finishing the large Paschal Candle stick that now stands beside the altar in our chapel, the texture of which I regularly feel as I recall the remarkable texture of Steve's own life. That, more than any other, is my "transitional object." But during those weeks I also turned more bowls, and did so more intensely, than at any other time, as far as I can recall. It was part of my journey into grief, part of my discovery of the mystery of being human in the face of death and in relation

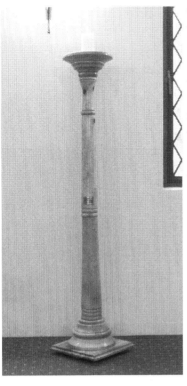

to the Source of all being—themes that I then began to explore in my book *Led into Mystery*.

I am indebted to the Catholic theologian Karl Rahner for the description of theology as being "led into mystery," and therefore the reminder that doing theology is not simply an academic exercise. It is an existential journey into the mystery of life and death, the mystery of the embodied soul being enfolded, yet always in relation to others in the mystery of God, who is infinite love and indescribable beauty. In Isobel's and my experience, owning grief is more than going through various steps from anger to acceptance; it was and always will be a painful, yet paradoxically enriching part of our journey, that we share with others in being led by God deeper into the mystery of who God is.

Your account of designing and making your table and of its significance for you also calls to mind the communion table I made for the Rondebosch United Church in Cape Town where I have spent much of my life as a member and honorary associate minister, and where Steve's own formation was so well shaped. It's also a church that you have inspired with your poetic and liturgical creativity. So I was not surprised when our current pastor, Robert Steiner, asked me to replace the oblong communion table with a round one. But instead I proposed one that was octagonal. This would equally enable the congregation to gather around the table, but it would have additional symbolism and, after all, I could not simply copy you or emulate your work!

There was some hesitation on Robert's part so I had to provide a rationale for an eight-sided communion table. In the back of my mind there was a good theological reason for such a table, but I decided to check it out on the web for starters. I discovered much of interest but little of significance for the task at hand. Then I recalled the old Sunday School question: "What did God do after he had rested on the seventh, or sabbath, day?" The eighth day of the week is, I now well know, the first day of the week, the Lord's Day, the day of resurrection and the gift of the Spirit. After a sabbath rest, God continued with the work of sustaining and growing the creation. In other words, God's creativity did not come to an end on Saturday. God took a sabbatical breather only to begin again the next day. As the Russian Orthodox philosopher Nicholas Berdyaev once said, "Creativeness in the world is, as it were, the eighth day of creation." An octagonal communion table reminds us that the church is a fellowship of those who share in God's continuing creation, nurture, and renewal of the world, and that God's gifts of bread and wine on the table are a means of God's grace in the ongoing task of the new creation.

I had already made several communion tables and altars for various churches, including the two chapels at Volmoed. Each was designed and made to fit into the style and character of the building. The first one, for the smaller Volmoed chapel we call the sanctuary, was made of camphor. I also turned the Paschal Candlestick out of a camphor log from the same tree as Bill Davis made the Christ figure. The second, for the Hermanus United Church, where I also made the baptismal font and lectern, was out of Canadian maple with rosewood inlays. The third was for the larger chapel at Volmoed. I made it of cottonwood with jacaranda edges, a rosewood inlay of the Volmoed cross in the center, and rosewood corners. I also made it square to match the shape of the building, and fitted hidden casters so that it could be easily moved for different styles of worship. If need be, you can dance round it more easily than a traditional altar!

The Rondebosch Church building by contrast with these others is a rather stately late Victorian edifice. It has very thick stone walls (no foundations to talk of!) and a high roof with gables and turrets. Inside, the walls are panelled in American oak, and much of the furniture, including the pews, is well made and shaped from the same wood. So it seemed appropriate that the new octagonal table should be made from oak as well. But as there are 600 varieties of oak, I had to make sure that the oak used for the table was American white. This links our church with the American forests, a reminder of our relationship to many friends across the Atlantic who have worshipped with us. Wood is universal; it knows no ethnic barriers.

Whatever its variety, oak has lasting qualities, which is why it was used to make the great sailing ships on which my grandfather lived and worked during the early part of his life; and it has symbolic meaning. In many cultures oak trees are sacred, the gateway between time and eternity. Incidentally, the first covenant made by Joshua with the Lord was under an oak tree (Josh 24:25–27). Yet, in spite of this rich history, oak is often dull and somber, so in making the octagonal table I decided to add additional color and symbolism. For the nine inlaid crosses, one on each side and one in the centre of the table, I used Maple, or *Acer*, which contrasted well with the oak. For the top edging of each side I used *Saligna* (Eucalyptus, or Blue

Gum), which is listed in South Africa as an invasive tree. This means that it should not be planted because it is a prodigious drinker of water. But it is a reminder that Jesus welcomes strangers to his table as much as those who are considered members, just as he ate with women, pub-owners, and others deemed unclean by the custodians of the religious laws of his day. In addition, he commanded his disciples to go into the highways and byways and bring to the table all those in need.

You may wonder how I got the angles of the top right. As you know, I have made round tables and, of course, cut them with a router just as you described, though for smaller ones I have used the bandsaw and my lathe. But an octagonal one? That was a problem, especially for someone who is mathematically challenged, but not for someone whose wife is a mathematician. So after deciding on the size of the table, I made it square to begin with, joining together several large pieces of oak that I had cut, planed, and prepared for biscuit-joining. I made sure that the grain of each piece matched the one alongside it, and they were all clearly marked to indicate where they belonged. By this stage Serghay had joined me in the process. So together we dry assembled the whole piece, that is, we did not glue it all together, but clamped it tight.

Next came the advanced mathematics. I called on Isobel. She soon worked out the angles that needed to be cut to make the square into an octagonal. I transferred these onto the square so that I now had the design in place and could see which pieces could now be glued together before cutting the angles. I did this because I wanted to cut them on my Festool miter-saw to ensure accuracy. But this meant that I could only cut a few joined planks at a time. An alternative would have been to use a power hand saw, or even a powerful jigsaw, but neither seemed right for the job. Like all good miter-saws, the Festool is amazing for this kind of work as you can set it to cut angles with absolute accuracy. But Serghay and I still decided to do some test cuts on other pieces of wood before proceeding. Then, once the cuts were made, we reassembled the sections (having carefully marked them beforehand, as I have said) and glued up. Of course, you have to have big enough clamps and lots of

space in which to work.

Then came the finishing—such a critical stage in the process of making anything worthwhile. You have described your technique in some detail. Let me just say a few words. I think the critical step in finishing is getting a well-planed surface that does not require much sandpapering. But sanding is invariably necessary, at least for my projects. Working through the grits from 80 (if need be) or better from 120 to a much finer 240 or even 320 is important. Depending on what I am making I normally use either Danish Teak oil or a polyurethane finish.

Guess you will stick to round tables, Bill?

•

I don't know, John. Now that I know the secret . . . and can call on Isobel . . . I might branch out. In any case, what strikes me here—amidst all this talk of tools, techniques, and wood—is that these tables we have made, like so much else, are places where memory is revived and created. Why don't we turn to that now?

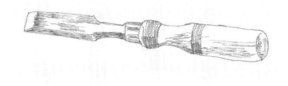

Remembering with Wood

Material Meditation

All this talk of tables for worship and the technical challenges they present reminds me, John, of what happens to me as I approach them. For instance, most of my projects involve some mortise and tenon work. I install a bit on my router whose diameter is the width of the mortise and then use a variety of jigs and templates, as well as my router guide, to cut the mortise to the depth I require. I then cut the tongue of the tenon on the table saw just shy of the desired thickness. And then I plane and file the tenon until it fits snugly in the mortise, with the shoulders of the tenon fitting tightly against the face of the mortise. It is an exacting and time-consuming procedure that leaves a swirl of sawdust and shavings on the floor.

In order to execute this task, as with many other similar procedures in the shop, I concentrate wholly on the task at hand. I don't play the radio or any music, not only because machine noise would drown out the sound, but in order to focus my mind. I have come to think of it as a kind of meditation that screens out the news bulletins, errand lists, unsolved family problems, and public policy debates that would otherwise force their way into my psyche. Some people speak of this process as "being in the flow." John Gernandt puts "Focus" at the top of his list of virtues for the woodworker. I have come to call it "material meditation." I never get much out of "staring into space" meditation, where I wrestle with my own mind, one phantom trying to pin another to the floor. Not even the yoga that I do to tame my sciatica has the same impact.

In fact, this form of meditation has been with me since I was a child. Working on my little Erector Set projects I recall almost going into a sort of trance in which it was only me and the steel parts, transforming a pile of metal into a windmill or a coal tipple. In material meditation, the mind is focused on the material at hand and in my hand. It is concentrated on the single motion of mind-muscle-hand-tool-material. The wood and the tool channel the bodily-mental energy toward a plan appropriate to the wood, with its own characteristics and internal forces. It's a form of meditation that can judge me with an injury, a marring of the wood, or a failure to execute a design. The meditation has a result that reflects back on my agency (unless the tool fails, of course) as well as on my possible failure to read the wood's grain, figure, or stability.

This kind of meditation is also as widespread as any craftwork, or for that matter, with any labor with natural materials. I think gardeners experience the same liberating focus and discipline of the senses. Perhaps we don't hear much about this because of the subtle aristocratic disparagement of craft and labor that accompanies some of the "loftier" spiritualities of immateriality. But in this focusing of my energies I experience a liberating sense of concentration and a sense of tangible incarnation, if you will. It brings a greater unity of spirit and body, and a confirming sense of being part of the world and contributing to its transformation. The point is not merely to quiet my mind and focus my spirit but to be engaged with the transformation of the world. In this way my whole bodily self is in greater resonance with the spirit continually at work in transforming the body of the universe. Maybe this is why Christian history has portrayed Jesus, the one filled with God's Spirit, as a woodworker. Maybe.

At the very least the tree and the cross are tied together in extraordinary ways in Christian memory. I think we even take it for granted that the center of our faith is tied so closely to a tree, indeed, nailed to it. And it's not just an accidental presence of the tree, since, as you have said earlier, it goes back deep into Jewish history. But I think it arises from the spirit of the tree itself. Sometimes I feel as drawn to identify with the trees as I am to my image of Jesus.

When we first bought land for our house here, it not only contained the stately tulip poplar but also was traversed by an old logging trail that wound up to a waterfall. Along the way stood some large basswood trees, prized by woodcarvers for its clear straight grain and medium density. A pair of them leaned out from the mountainside. I wondered then how long

they would be able to stand amid our storms and seasons. When one of
them fell last year it made a powerful impact on me, as if I had fallen with it.

Last night the basswood fell
    clean across the trail to the waterfall.
For twenty years we watched it leaning,
    roots hidden underneath the humus of ten thousand falls,
    locked within the splintered mantle of our mountain.
With every annual ring it yielded to the pull of earth
    until it rested in the arms of slender buckeyes and a cherry tree.
Holding it they danced five winters,
    let their leaves play in palpitation,
    changed their dress from mossy green to calico
    before they fell in trusting premonition.
The night was still
    when its time came.
I with every creature heard it
    when the cherry and the buckeye
    received the basswood's death,
    and in embrace
    they fell together
    in our way.

In Celebration of Olive Wood

Bill, your experience and your poem reminded me of that day I mentioned
earlier when I arrived home to discover a pile of freshly cut wild olive wood
on my doorstep. This had never happened before, even though, as you know
from your visits to Volmoed, olive trees are plentiful in our valley. From our
house you can see row after row on the nearby hills. These are planted and
cultivated for their fruit, as are those in most Mediterranean countries—
whose climate is much like ours. The oldest olive tree is believed to be more
than two thousand years old, like the one on the Mount of Olives outside the
walls of Jerusalem reputed to have been there in Jesus' day. Wild olive trees

in South Africa are usually scattered on farms and the veld, on hill slopes or in glens providing shade and giving the area character. But they are seldom cut down or blown over by the wind. So when some large chunks become available on rare occasions I consider myself very fortunate.

Olive is very hard, heavy, and dense, and this lot was no exception, as my chainsaw discovered when cutting the pieces into manageable chunks. Like most hardwoods, olive has to be wet to turn; otherwise it is impossible to gouge out the inside. What I love about olive is its magnificent grain, which ranges in color from a deep brown to yellow. It is extravagant and exuberant. This gives each piece a unique beauty. You don't make furniture from olive wood, but it is wonderful for smaller items: candle sticks, cutting boards, and various sizes of platters and bowls. Apart from turning a few smaller items, some candlesticks amongst them, from the logs I received that day, I also turned a much larger bowl—the biggest olive bowl I have ever seen.

Because olive is so hard, my turning tools had to be particularly sharp to make a worthwhile impression on it. But the log I had been given was not only hard and dense, it was also unusually large. This presented a major challenge, as it had to be cut and shaped first of all with a chainsaw and roughly rounded in order to be balanced when placed on the lathe. It was slow work. Serghay and I finally managed to get it right, attached to a face-plate and loaded onto the lathe. But even then, reasonably balanced, it was a fearsome sight as the lathe began to turn and the wood gathered speed. Serghay watched from a distance! My first task was to cut through the bark. Only then would I discover what lay beneath and whether this rough piece of wood held out some promise of producing a bowl worthy of all the effort. I was not disappointed! As I cut beneath the surface the most amazing grain appeared with, to quote my friend Mary again, a "surprising innate loveliness." My thoughts instantly went back to our son Steve. That load of olive wood that arrived on my doorstep was becoming a sign of grace, an assurance of hope, a gift in remembrance of Steve and the wonderful grain that his life revealed.

During the three years before his tragic death in February 2010, Steve, a professor of theology at the University of KwaZulu-Natal, was developing what he called "olive theology." Using the olive as a metaphor for the relationship between theology, economic ethics, and ecology, Steve spoke of "An Olive Agenda"

in doing theology, in which he brought together theologies of justice and freedom with eco-theology. For him, peace *on* earth meant also peace *with* the earth. Not surprisingly he soon found himself in creative dialogue with Palestinian Christians and theologians for whom the olive tree is such a poignant and powerful symbol of their struggle for land and life. So it was that the first Steve de Gruchy Memorial Lecture given by Desmond Tutu in 2012 celebrated Steve's "olive theology"; while the third, in June 2014, by the Palestinian theologian Mitri Raheb, perceptively wove the various strands in Steve's thought together in the context of the Palestinian struggle. Isobel did likewise in a poem she wrote for the first lecture.

When I think olive, I think colour,
the green of leaves mixed with the brown of earth,
not a lush green, not a rich earth,
but dulled down, dusty, khaki,
colour of South Africa, colour of Africa,
colour of the Middle East.
When I think green I think green issues;
save the environment, save the rhino,
save the forests, save the wetlands:
when I think brown, I think brown issues;
dryness, drought,
lack of water, lack of food,
struggle for survival, save the people.
Which comes first, which takes precedence?
When I think olive, I think brown and green together—
integrate, adapt, survive and thrive.

When I think olive I think fruit,
oily, bitter, black or greenish,
not to be picked and eaten from the tree,
like some round, red juicy apple,
but shaken, gathered, processed,
watched over, worked over, waited over,
to produce small, salty mouthfuls,
more pip than flesh,
but satisfying, even desired, food.
I think life is like that,
easy pickings mean very little;
what counts comes from watching, working, waiting.

When I think olive I think oil,
pressed in family presses, in community mills,
yellow gold, tasty and rich;
but more than that, health giving,
not oil that hardens arteries, clogs veins,
deposits fat,
but fruit and oil maintaining health.

When I think olive I think tree,
I think row upon row of trees,
stretching up and over hills, rocky and dry,
narrow leaves, fluttering, now silver, now green,
in the breeze, casting dappled shadows.
Trees mean life—more oxygen,
more soil retention,
more shelter for other creatures,
and trees point to the sacred in life,
in every culture, people, time:
their majesty, their size,
their longevity, their beauty;
all take us beyond ourselves to the Creator.

When I think olive I think age upon age,
the olive trees in Gethsemane,
the same Jesus prayed under,
twisted, gnarled trunks, porous, and cracked,
dead to our eyes, but able to resprout, to resurrect:
trees that talk of survival over drought, storm, time,
providing food for each generation
that comes and goes,
lives and dies,
wages war, works for peace.

When I think olive, I think olive branch,
I think peace, and I almost despair.
Who comes today carrying the olive branch?
Rather they come ripping out the trees,
destroying the ancient olive groves,
tearing apart communities,
destroying livelihoods, destroying peoples,
in Palestine, in Africa, in communities,
in families—in ourselves,
unless we think olive branch,
think peace, wage peace.

When I think olive, and I think the Bible,
Noah, his dove, and his olive branch,
The oil running down Aaron's beard,
The oil of anointing, the Chosen One, king or priest,
The Anointed One, the Messiah,
The olive tree, used by God as a symbol of peace,
Of well-being for body, soul and spirit,
Of Shalom, of salaam,
Made one in Christ, the Anointed One,
Truly human, truly God,
To make us fully human and God-like.

When I think Olive I think Steve,
His life, his work, his death,
His gifts, his legacy, his Olive Theology.
I think Steve,
And I almost despair,
But the olive points to life,
To survival, to the next generation,
to the next ones chosen
to bear the olive branch, to do theology—
to do Olive Theology.

~

Balance

Isobel's poem, along with your reflections on the Olive and mine on the Basswood, intensify for me the awareness of how our memory and our emotions are tied to wood. Maybe we can apply new meanings to the old saw about "knocking on wood" and tapping our knuckles to our head! But now I want to return to your octagonal table of the new creation and an issue that has been important for me.

Your table looks pretty solid sitting on its heavy base, and I know it is, because I've had the privilege of worshipping around it. But this achievement was not so easy for my round table with its two drop-leaves and double gate-legs! The fundamental problem was how to make the table both narrow, so it could function more as an altar against the wall, as well as wide enough so it could create a circle of people with the leaves extended. The double gate-leg design solves that problem by extending supports wide of the sides. But in subsequent round tables I moved beyond the gate-leg de-sign to other means of supporting the drop-leaves. By the time I did a communion table for Boston University School of Theology I devised some sliding dovetail extension arms. This threatened the stability of the table even more and posed the central question more starkly—how do you achieve balance in a world of gravitation?

Balance is not merely the physical problem encountered by a walker on a tightrope (it gives me vertigo just to think of those daredevils), but also a perceptual problem of form, proportion, and pleasing appearance. Something can *look* tippy even if it resists the forces of gravity. This is a challenge not only of recalling my high school physics, but of training the eye as well as the inner ear.

Shortly after completing the table for Andover Newton, my friend Tom Porter, with whom I had worked on restorative justice and conflict resolution programs, asked me to build a round table as the focus for worship shaped by the circle processes of reconciliation. It came to be called the JustPeace Table, named for the United Methodist organization Tom founded for these purposes.

For Tom, the dynamic of reconciliation found in circle processes arises from the baptismal powers given to every Christian. This dynamic draws from a well of spiritual power that Tom spelled out in some detail. So I decided that the pedestal would replicate a traditional well, with four legs arching to a point above the center. This led me to a heavy base of walnut posts, held together by a circular piece of cherry near the base. The top of the shared arc would have to be flattened to provide enough leverage to balance the circular fixed top. Too little, and the top would look insecure. Too much, and the arch would be destroyed. Moreover, the width of the top would have to be proportional to the distance between the legs.

Taking all these factors into account resulted in dimensions hovering around the famous Golden Proportion of 1 to 1.6 that has informed the eye of designers throughout the ages. There is a connection between our sense of harmony and the actual physical characteristics of our world. Ed Davis,

who has made a good deal of church furniture, says that "Wood-work is material music." The same harmonies that apply to beautiful sound apply also to the work made of wood. Now, this is nothing new. Pythagoras and his followers famously joined physics and aes-thetics, matter and beauty, in their teachings 2500 years ago. (Of course, the mathematics of gravity had to wait for Isaac Newton, only to be relativized by Albert Einstein in our own time.) But here I was rediscovering them in the actual trial and error of achieving both balance and beauty in the same object—a table that would evoke the circle processes of reconciliation.

Thus, I was exploring the relation of the universe's physical proper-ties with our sense of beauty and our experience of evoking balance and harmony among people. Here I was at the crossroads of truth, beauty, and goodness—the path of philosophers and theologians for centuries. But this was not a speculative reach of my reason. It was the result of working with wood to coax it into a durable and useful object that was pleasing to the eye and hand.

In working out these problems I recalled that I had gone off to college intent on being a mathematics major. It only took me one semester of in-creasing consternation to realize that my love of calculus and geometry had been inspired by a teacher, Edward Smith, who would complete a theorem on the blackboard, turn around toward us, his face beaming, and say exul-tantly, "Now isn't that beautiful!" I thought it was the logic of the equations that had caught my imagination, but it was the elegance of its forms. When I got to college mathematics, what I was really looking for was the forms and the materiality that expressed them. Now I realize that what I was looking for was the wood, the material, the concrete reality in which mathematics is embedded.

And I think that puts it right. Most of our Western spirituality is an attempt to transcend the material world in order to commune, somehow, with the invisible "idea" or "form" beyond it. We tend to think that the "idea" is primary and shapes the world. What I have been doing with wood is to reverse this order and priority. It is this very "thingness" that is my life, the grain and growth of it, the resilience and the splintering. Ideas are a response, an effort to order, to guide my action. But it is the life of the wood that I respect and to which I am responding. Through it I become, quite literally, "grounded" and "rooted." The tree yields the metaphors, not for a "higher" reality, but for how I am to fully live in this creation.

By calling these things around me a "creation" I open up this material reality to wider dimensions and possibilities that go far beyond my imagination. By calling it "creation" I acknowledge that it can and does reveal more than my intentions granted it. And in touching it, working with it, listening to it, I find a flow of energy that enlivens me, even when my body grows tired.

Well, this was about balance. But balance is also about standing, about being properly grounded in relationship to the forces around us. It means taking account of what is inherent in the earth, its gravity, the proportions that are fitting to our sensibilities. It means, as the Navajo have said, "walking in beauty."

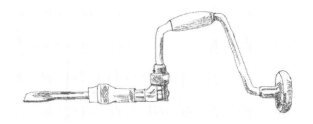

Meanings In Wood

Fonts, Lecterns, and a Crosier

"Walking in Beauty," "Building in Beauty." The phrases remind me, Bill, of Dietrich Bonhoeffer's remark in his *Letters and Papers from Prison* that the recovery of aesthetic existence in the church was important for its renewal. Attention to aesthetics, utility, and meaning have certainly all been in my mind when working on things I have built for use in worship.

The first was a large baptismal font I turned out of maple and African rosewood for the Hermanus United Church, matching the communion table and lectern that I also made when the church was renovated. Fortu-nately the headstock of my lathe could turn on its base, enabling me to load the large pieces of maple, roughly cut round for balance, onto the chuck facing towards me rather than the bed. I turned the bowl by building up layers one on top of the next, and turning each as I did so. This, incidentally, is the same tech-nique used for turning segmented bowls. The result, I thought, was quite stunning. The stem, also maple, was turned in sections but as a spindle. And then the base, which had to be as large as the bowl and heavy enough to keep the font steady, was turned in sections on the chuck much like the bowl itself.

The next font, for a Methodist Church in London, England, was made in the same way. It, too, was a large piece of work. The reason I was asked to make it was that someone had donated money for a font made out of African indigenous wood by someone who lived in Africa. In the end I chose kiaat for this purpose as it has a beautiful texture and grain (deep brown to yellow)—though the sawdust I must say is highly toxic, a danger facing all wood turning projects of this kind. I must add that the cost of transporting the font from my workshop to London in a ship's container was far in excess of what it cost to make or the pay that I received, generous as that was.

The third font was made for the chapel at the Diocesan School for Boys (locally called "Bishops") in Cape Town. This, too, was an unexpected commission. It was smaller than the others, intended for the old and smaller chapel, made out of white oak, and square in design. In all three I inlaid some appropriate symbols.

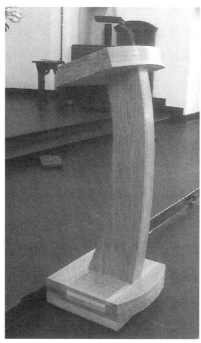

The first of the lecterns was, as I have said, made for the Hermanus United Church, and like the table and the font, made out of maple and rosewood. As the church had long since dispensed with its pulpit, the lectern was designed not only for the reading of the Bible but also for preaching. The challenge again was stability, getting the height and angles correct, and making sure that it was well designed, with an appropriate dignity and beauty.

The second lectern was more of a challenge. This was commissioned once again by Bishops' School in Cape Town, but for the large and impressive chapel where the boys assemble regularly for Morning Prayers. Once again, because the lectern was intended to serve as a pulpit (the existing pulpits being totally inappropriate), it had to be easily moveable and therefore, because of its size and weight, have wheels. And, as the chaplain told me, it had to have a modern shape that would be attractive for teenage boys and yet fit into the rather Italianate decor and design of the building!

I once again chose white oak for the task. In order to achieve the sweeping arch-like design I made a template (drawn by Isobel) cut on my band saw. Serghay and I then joined eight pieces of oak into four equal pieces wide enough to be cut according to the template and long enough for the height of the stem. We then cut the four sections following the template and laminated them together. The curves were later cleaned up with a spokeshave, power sander, and hand sanding. The bottom of the laminated stem was long enough so that we could cut a large tenon, which went into the base where it was glued in place and bolted from underneath. The tricky bit was ensuring that it was all well balanced once the top was fixed onto the stem. The rest was plain sailing. Of course, I had to make an appropriately heavy base to make sure it would not fall over, especially during a lively service conducted by teenage boys. I thought when I finished the lectern that I had probably completed making furniture for Anglicans. But a further ecumenical project was already on the horizon.

When Margaret Vertue, the new Anglican Bishop of False Bay, Cape Town, asked me to make her crosier, I was delighted, yet daunted by the challenge. A crosier, so the *Oxford Dictionary of the Christian Church* tells us, is the "crook-shaped staff of bishops," which began to be used in liturgical ceremonies in the seventh century. The original design used in the Eastern Orthodox Church, and still used today, was a staff "surmounted by a cross between two serpents." This referred back to Moses holding up a staff with a serpent embellished on it during the wilderness journey of the Israelites as a sign of healing. "So Moses made a serpent of bronze and put it upon a pole; and whenever a serpent bit someone, that person would look at the serpent of bronze and live" (Num 21:9).

The serpent, the symbol of evil, had become transformed into one of healing. Centuries later Jesus referred to this ancient event in speaking of his death. "Just as Moses lifted up the serpent in the wilderness, so must the Son of Man be lifted up, that whoever believes in him may have eternal life" (John 3:14). So it was appropriate that the Patriarchs of the Eastern Church should carry a staff in which the cross is at the centre of the serpents, the sign of God's suffering love and redemptive power over evil. Most people today who observe a bishop carrying a crosier of this description probably do not understand its significance. This is especially so in the West where the form of the crosier came to resemble a shepherd's crook, symbolizing the pastoral role of the bishop as the shepherd of the flock. Even though crosiers are not part of my tradition I think the symbolism is rich, whether in its more ancient form or that with which we might be more familiar.

But the crosier also took on another meaning during the Middle Ages. Often made of silver and gold and embellished with precious stones, it became a symbol of episcopal power, often to the detriment of its significance as a sign of God's healing love revealed in the suffering of Jesus, or the bishop's role as pastor of the pastors and shepherd of the flock. To make such a crosier would not only have challenged my craftsmanship beyond possibility, but also transgressed my conscience comfort zone. Fortunately, Bishop Margaret had other ideas. "Keep it simple, light, and just like a shepherd's crook should be!"

As the crosier has to be used by the bishop as she travels around her large diocese and even further afield, quite apart from being carried by her during countless ceremonies, it not only had to be reasonably light, but also strong, and divided into three sections so that it could be easily dismantled and reassembled. I was also asked to make a case in which it could be carried, something sturdy but also manageable. For the crosier itself, I decided on beech, with inlaid purpleheart at the joints. For the case, I chose high quality pine. Beech is white, has straight grain making it strong, and is comparatively light; purpleheart is beautiful and appropriately episcopal in color; pine, especially of good quality, is unpretentious, sturdy, inexpensive, and finishes well with several coats of polyurethane varnish.

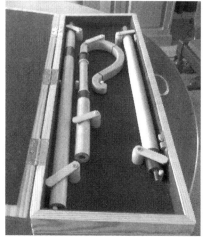

Making the staff in three sections was straightforward and easily done on the lathe, though the measurements had to be precise. Making the crook at the top was a different story. Here I called again on the mathematical expertise of Isobel, who worked out the angles for three blocks of wood to be joined together so that the grain would run straight even though the wood appeared to be bent back on itself. Once the three pieces were cut on my miter-saw—which makes cutting obscure angles simply a pleasure—and joined together with dowels, I was then able to trace on the design of the crook and cut it to shape on the bandsaw. Further shaping was then done by hand using a spokeshave, rasp, and carving tools.

The next challenge was to work out how to join the three sections of the staff together so that they could be easily taken apart and yet, when joined, would be strong enough to withstand the rigorous use to which the finished product would be put. A visit to a specialist hardware store solved that problem, providing me with the necessary fittings. Woodworkers owe much to the knowledge of those who work in hardware stores, especially if they are craftsmen or women themselves and know what you are talking about, but equally to those who design exactly what you need for the job in the first place, probably—no, definitely—never expecting them to be used in making a bishop's crook!

~

From Crutch to Cross

Wood, as you have just shown John, is a powerful symbolic medium—the curve reaching upward, the distortions leading us beyond our comforts, the figure reminding us of deeper meanings. Whether it is the tree of Buddhist enlightenment, the trees of Mamre or Lebanon in the Old Testament, or the rough cross of Christianity, wood has a peculiar capacity to express our symbolic needs. Sometimes it is the character of the wood itself, as when our own struggle for life is expressed in its figure and grain, often contorted by the stress of wind or drought. Wood is pliable; it can be fashioned into so many forms. And, as I recounted in my reflection on building the communion table, the very act of transforming the wood transforms us as well.

A few years ago, Beth Follum Hoffman participated in a workshop with me and others on "Wood, Rocks, and Worship" at Andover Newton Theological School. We had asked participants to bring some wood that was significant to them and that they wanted to work with in the course of the week. Beth brought a pair of old wooden crutches. She had been born with one leg shorter than the other and it had only been through years of painful surgery and therapy that she was now able to walk unassisted by the crutches, which she had stored some years ago in her attic. The course requirement led her to take them out, knowing that these maple crutches were very important but not knowing what she would do with them.

In the course of the workshop she transformed these crutches in a way that transformed her in the process. Despite her complete lack of experience with woodworking tools, she discovered that "I had a lot to say to the wood and . . . the wood also had a lot to say to me." She decided, with the support, help, and encouragement of the other participants, to re-fashion them into something significant that would be a third life for the maple tree and would reflect the painful journey she had experienced in her own life.

As she went back and forth between her own experience and the actual shape of the wooden pieces, she began to see a way the crutches might become a cross. In the process, she confronted her own struggle to absorb her traumatic childhood experience and refashion it so it might provide a language and symbolism for her own emerging ministry amid the myriad

forms of brokenness and healing she was encountering in the lives of people in her church. At the end emerged a cross that clearly reflected its earlier form but in a new arrangement that would absorb its old meanings into a more universal symbol of suffering and new life. She didn't build a base for it, but wanted it to hang over the very table I talked about earlier. It would dance in the air, just as her spirit was lifting her own body, and with it the spirits of everyone who gathered around the table on our final day together for communion. It remains one of the most moving experiences with wood in my own life and in hers.

Through the work of our hands and our imagination, our dialogue with wood can transform us as well as the wood. In doing so, we contribute to the transformation of others as well. I have heard it said that healing is the work of the hands, but the realization that wood can be a powerful intermediary in this process was never so clear as in Beth's transformation of her crutches into a cross of resurrection. Beth is now a minister in Maine, where the cross hangs in her office as a sign to everyone of the transformation that is possible in their lives.

The Healing Serpent

It was not long afterward that I made a very different cross. Now here, with your story of the crosier, is a place where we arrived at a very similar point by coincidence. One day Sylvia returned from a walk in the woods above our house to tell me she had seen a young tree with a vine wound so tight around it that the tree itself had taken on the serpentine shape of the vine's impress. I had just received an inquiry from Andover Newton about making a processional cross that could accompany the other pieces I had made for them. Immediately I thought of a cross that would recall the serpent that

Moses lifted up to save his people—an image, as you pointed out, later used by St. John to speak of Jesus' crucifixion. So we went back to the tree she had spotted on her walk. We soon agreed it had enough size and straightness to support the cross, so we cut it down and took it back home.

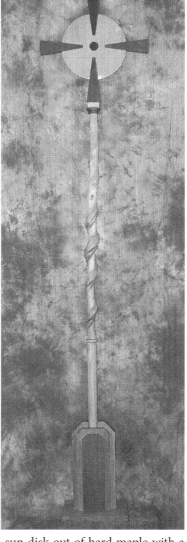

As I proceeded with stripping the vine and the bark from the slender trunk, I was aware that I could have used a piece of wood from the lumberyard, dried in a kiln, and cut at the mill. But it felt very different to allow two plants simply to reveal what they had created in the woods on their own. As I stripped the bark from the wood I could see and feel how the tree, a local species of maple, had actually grown into the space allowed by the constricting vine. Of course, I would have to let the air dry it a while, but this organic expression of an ancient religious symbol somehow made it more real, more powerful. I think that is why we work with these natural and found materials. They convey a power from beyond us—one we respond to and which brings us into a conversation we didn't create on our own.

Once the staff was ready, I had to decide on the design for the cross it would support. I decided to create a sun disk out of hard maple with a center of purpleheart (what would we theologian woodworkers do without purpleheart!) to reflect the bloody reality of the cross. After I turned the disk, I made four rays of walnut that would reflect the dawning power of resurrection, thus bringing together the themes of the healing serpent, the sacrificial death of Jesus, and the new power that flooded into the world.

Like you, I had to figure out how to make it something that could be disassembled for shipping. Attaching the proper fittings was perhaps the hardest part of the whole project. A colleague at Andover Newton had to make adjustments to it even after it reached the school.

Because of the slender character of the serpentine staff—the heart of its power, I think—it has the quality of a reed waving in the wind. Maybe this is Isaiah's "bruised reed" that the Suffering Servant will not break, just as he will not extinguish a flickering lamp (Isa 42:3). But for me it is more like the willow or any supple tree that bends in the wind rather than break in defiant rigidity. It is a piece whose intertwined woods bring together many symbolic dimensions, even as it posed some technical challenges that tested and expanded my own abilities.

~

Safety First!

Your talk about testing your abilities, Bill, reminds me that we haven't said much here about the need to pay proper attention to safety while we work with all these sharp and powerful tools. Now that is where we need the "material meditation" and "focus" you talked about earlier! Let me just recount my story about how I learned this lesson.

In February 2014, I badly cut three of my fingers on my jointer. I don't have to remind you that this is a powerful and, like others, potentially dangerous machine for planing one side of a piece of wood perfectly flat. Its cutter, about twelve inches long, spins around at a high speed shaving the wood as you pass it over the revolving blade. It was late in the afternoon after a busy day at a time when I should have been relaxing, but instead I decided to plane a large piece of wood, larger than I should have on my jointer, and to do so without the help of the push-stick I had recently designed and made especially for it. What makes this even more inexplicable was that earlier in the day I had demonstrated its use to Serghay and stressed the importance of using it! All of a sudden as the wood passed over the cutter it was wrenched from my hands and my fingers were dragged onto the blades. Blood spurted out of the cuts, spilling onto the machine and the floor. I desperately tried to stop the bleeding with a tissue, then rushed into the house leaving a trail of blood on the path, the front door, and kitchen floor. Isobel immediately ran to my aid when I shouted out, helped staunch the bleeding, and then rushed me down to the Medi-clinic.

I was soon in the emergency ward under the care of the sister-in-charge. Then our doctor and the surgeon on duty arrived and two hours later my fingers were stitched. I was on pain-killers and antibiotics, and our mutual friend and director of Volmoed, Bernhard Turkstra, arrived to take me home. It was bad, but it could have been a lot worse. I could visualize what might have happened to my hands, and what might have happened if there was no clinic within fifteen minutes drive, no professionals to do what they did, no medicines, no drugs to ease the pain. I had made a stupid mistake in trying to do what I did when I did it. I had broken the basic rules of workshop safety and was paying the penalty, even though I had actually got off reasonably lightly. But within a few days I was back in my workshop, even though my injured fingers were still heavily bandaged. "I see you got back on your horse!" remarked Bernhard with his usual insight. Or, as my father used to say when I was learning to ride my bicycle: "If you fall off, get back on straightaway, otherwise you will never learn." Important counsel for the journey of life.

So what did I learn from my mishap in the workshop? For one thing, it could have been much worse! Not everyone can say that about their afflictions because for many people it can't get any worse and they are understandably crushed. But sometimes in our afflictions we need to count our blessings, to get them into perspective lest they crush us. We need to remember to get back on our bicycle as soon as possible! I also learnt that even when you are supposed to be experienced, full of wisdom, and even called the sage on the hill, you can act stupidly. Nobody needs to tell me about safety in the workshop. I know the rules and every handbook for every tool reminds me about them. But that did not prevent me from disobeying them. As we grow older we have an abundance of experience to draw on. But experience also teaches us that the lessons of life have to be learnt again and again. Otherwise we might also lose our souls.

•

My fingers winced as you recounted that story, John. Woodwork is mindfulness every moment. To help me I now have stickers in my shop. One at the lathe, says "Remember Ron" in order to remind me to observe safety rules as I approach it. Now I have added one to my jointer that says "Remember John" in order to remind me to always use my push stick there. I have another "Remember John" (my friend John Gernandt) to remind me about table-saw safety. Pretty soon all my machines will have memorials attached to them! Admonitions to mindfulness need a little help. There must be a connection here between Buddhism, with its call to mindfulness, and woodworking. Consider the intermixture of Japanese Shinto and

Buddhism that must be feeding into their great tradition of woodworking and tool-making.

But your story reminds me of another side of this, and that's our Christian preoccupation, at least in our own heritage, with St. Paul's lament that we do what we know we shouldn't do and we don't do what we know we should do. Between will and way lies a great abyss. Somehow, we have to bridge the gap, not by grace alone, but by a good dose of common sense and respect for our machines before we lose any more fingers. But enough of this, lest, as you earlier warned when speaking about the toxicity of sawdust, we scare anyone off from this marvelous activity.

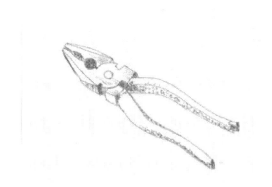

Connecting with Wood

Now that your hand has healed and I've added a "Remember John" to my jointer, let's turn to something we've mentioned all along—the way woodworking is a kind of connectivity, not just to the natural world but to other people. Whether people call it cabinetry, joinery, or simply furniture-making, it's all the same—woodworking that connects pieces together to create a structure made up of many pieces. And of course, we haven't even mentioned in this list the woodturning that has reached dazzling levels of artistry in our own time, often using a multiplicity of woods and other materials joined in complex ways. How you fit pieces of wood together so that they are strong, can adjust to seasonal wood movement, and yet be graceful and pleasing to the eye—that's the task. And we both have done a lot of it—mortise and tenon, dovetails, lapped joints, and more. In working the wood into proper connection, whether it is a segmented bowl or spindle, table, or chest, we need to understand what the wood is capable of and what we are capable of. We get connected with the wood and with ourselves at that level.

But this is not merely an isolated conversation. I am also thinking about who will use this table, this lectern, this chest of drawers. I am connected to those who will gather round this table, who will see in its inlays, figure, or shape some symbol of a larger world, some invitation to a larger life. The wood is getting a second life at our hands, enabling it to become a beautiful and useful object to enhance our life.

And so I have built a table to honor the memory of a woodworker alumnus of Andover Newton Theological School, choosing the woods he loved and trying to reflect something of his spirit. There are wall sconces for sculptures by my friend Charles McCollough. A bed, a table, and now a desk for my son Eric. Side tables for my daughter Aneliese. A bowl for my daughter Elaine. A dresser for my wife Sylvia. And I have gone on to build round communion tables for a hospital, a Methodist Conference headquarters, and several churches. And you have a long list like this as well. Virtually everything I have made—except my own desk and printer table!—has been for someone. This is a great gift, since most of us are consumed for most of our lives with doing things for an abstract clientele of customers, distant buyers, passing clients, and faceless institutions. While the erasure of craft connections has made possible enormous efficiencies, it has also separated us from each other and separated our relationships from tangible, durable materials. I feel it as a great loss and therefore a great privilege to nurture this need for material connection in our world today.

My younger daughter Elaine isn't a woodworker, but this value seems to have taken root in her own life as well. She recently wrote me that:

> I think what I've taken away as a lesson from my Dad's wood-working is the value of working with your hands. When my husband was in law school he read an old case to me which used the phrase "brain toiler." However amusing that phrase may be, it occurs to me that more and more we have become a nation of "brain toilers" and have lost a sense of connection to what is made with human hands.
>
> The importance of working with one's hands goes beyond what is produced. What is made can be shared and the giver and receiver are enriched. This is why I like gardening so much. Gardening is my way of working with my hands. It turns out that what is done slowly and with a sense of pride feeds the spirit and fosters community.
>
> My husband may not have much time to work with his hands these days, but he does have time to appreciate what is made by the hands of others. He can sit down at the table and enjoy some produce we receive through a share in a local farm which is served in a wooden bowl that was lovingly crafted by my dad.

Well, I'm glad that bowl has found some use and doesn't just sit on a shelf gathering dust! But it's not just that kind of usefulness that connects us. I think also about how a table that will be used in worship will also arrange a space in which people are related to each other in specific ways, whether it is to gather around a table, listen to someone at a pulpit or lectern, or, as you have done, gather for a baptism. And, of course, there are chairs. Grand cathedral chairs, regal thrones, elegant dining chairs, office chairs—a seemingly endless variety. And there are chairs for inspiration as well as use, like Sam Maloof's rockers or George Nakishima's elegantly balanced chairs. But I don't do chairs. First of all, if you build a chair, it usually means you have to make six of them to go around a table. Unless you're asked to build a Bishop's chair. I haven't been asked. So I've specialized in other things.

Most of us don't do everything. But I do remember how we built a couple of Adirondack chairs on my most recent visit to Volmoed.

•

Yes, indeed, Bill, that was a highlight of your recent stay and a great adventure in woodworking! Ever since Isobel, Steve, and I spent a summer in Stockbridge, Massachusetts back in 1964, when I was the supply pastor at the First Congregational Church (UCC), and had first seen and sat in an Adirondack, I had a longing to have one someday. As I anticipated your coming to Volmoed and therefore our next big joint woodworking project, I decided that now, fifty years later, was the time! So you kindly obtained the plans from *Fine Woodworking* (in inches!) and sent them to me so that I could buy the wood before your arrival.

I purchased unplaned rough pine, straight and true, enough for two chairs, and Serghay and I planed them in advance. Then you and Sylvia arrived, and the fun began! Interpreting the plans, detecting some minor (but significant nevertheless) mistakes in them, jumping between inches and centimeters, debating how best to proceed—with Serghay amused by our banter and antics, but also adding his own insight to the process—cutting, shaping, and sanding the pieces, and then assembling, gluing, screwing. The cutting at times was tricky because of the angles of some pieces, but there was no need for inlays or anything to add significance to what we were doing—the beauty was in the design and functionality, and the anticipation of comfort. Then came the finishing with four coats of an outdoor polyurethane varnish. Yes, the chairs had to be well sealed as they were intended for our verandah, which receives strong sunshine during summer and much rain during winter. Then within a day or two of your leaving we could all stand back and admire our handiwork, and sit in some style with a cup of coffee resting on the nice broad arm rests. Three cheers for whoever designed and built the first Adirondack chair!

Our own connection in this project gets me thinking about all the connections that have emerged through the work I've been doing with Serghay. A request from the Volmoed Art Group to make six wooden easels for use in the art studio was the incentive that launched Serghay and me to start working together in earnest. It also tied in with Volmoed's capacity-building policy to enable those employed on the ground and maintenance staff to be given additional skills training in some area, and also to earn extra income. So the Volmoed Woodworking Co-op was born. And since then, now only two years ago, we have made a fair amount of items for sale: work tables for the art studio, tables made from wine barrels for our gallery tea room, cutting and cheese boards, lamp stands, a blanket chest, and most recently a four-poster double bed! And no sooner has one project ended than another appears on the horizon. Each project is a learning experience for both of us, and a great pleasure at the same time.

Serghay and I particularly enjoy the challenge of bespoke items, for each one demands special attention, so we have lots of conversation about how we will approach the task. And at each stage we take a deep breath, stand back a while, and  consider the next step. You have described something of the process, Bill, and how you think through each phase as you lie in bed trying to go to sleep! I know exactly what you mean. It's better than counting sheep in order to get to sleep, and I often wake up in the morning with greater clarity on the next step or two.

Thinking further about connections brings to mind that I have probably made more coffee tables over the years than any other item of furniture, each one specially designed for some client, friend, or family member, though each different in design. I often think of them, where they are now located, and about those who gather around them like the one I made for Jeanelle's apartment in London.

She recently wrote to remind me how we had offered to buy a coffee table for her new London apartment. She had found one that fitted the bill—wood and glass, sleek and functional. In her account,

> Dad had a look and promptly pronounced that he'd replicate one for us—and I could transport it back to the UK with me on the plane. My partner, Heidi, looked dubious and made dissuading noises, while mom and I knew that dad could work out how to make it happen! So a few months later, there I was transporting back to the UK an ingeniously constructed coffee table base folded into an aircraft-friendly package. One glass table top later and we have a modern, stylish addition to our home—and a beautiful reminder of my Dad's generosity and skill.

Sometimes my impulsive offers give me the biggest challenges!

But the one I treasure most is an imbuia coffee table with a chessboard inlay for our own home. This has a very special significance for me. Steve and I played our last game of chess on it a month before he tragically died. Needless to say, he checkmated me! Since then, David, his son, and I have had some good contests as well, with the scores now probably even. So the table connects us three together across the generations in a very tangible way, evoking memories of Steve's last visit, and providing moments of bonding with my grandson when he stays with us.

Most items I make are for people I know, but sometimes commissions literally arrive on my doorstep with the unexpected arrival of a perfect stranger! One afternoon a few years after moving to Volmoed, an antique Bentley car pulled up outside my workshop. An elderly gentleman got out as I went out to see who was visiting. He said that he had heard I made furniture and wondered if I would make something special for him. He was rebuilding a 1915 Silver Cloud Rolls Royce, he told me, and needed a battery box that would be secured to the left hand side running board. It had to be made of teak with brass fittings, joined with finger joints, have a hinged lid, and be big enough to hold two batteries. As I was a sucker for such challenges I agreed, though I was by no means sure I could do what he was asking. "Where would I find Burmese teak?" I asked, as a possible escape route. He opened the trunk of his Bentley and there, stashed inside, were at least two dozen large teak planks that he had taken from a disused garage door. They were not in good shape, but teak is teak, and I knew that with some careful planing they would be just fine. In any case they had to be reduced to three eights of an inch for the job. I should have asked him, of course, how much he was willing to pay, but that slipped my mind when I agreed. The project was a great success and the pay was far in excess of what I had anticipated.

•

Yes, indeed, John, every piece has a memory and a story, it seems, but as you say, some are more poignant than others. Your account of the significance of your chess table reminds me that our mutual friend Peter Storey told me about a moving experience he had involving his grandfather's cabinet. Here's what he wrote:

> My paternal grandfather—whom I never knew because he died long before I was born—was a cabinet-maker from the English Lake District who came to South Africa to join the Methodist

ministry. There stood in my childhood home a tall, beautifully proportioned display cabinet, dark with decades of furniture oil, which he had made. When I ultimately inherited it I decided to give it a deep cleaning to reveal the original glow of the golden brown teak beneath. First I had to remove its doors, so, with the cabinet lying on its back, I found myself selecting one of my grandfather's old wooden-handled screwdrivers, and kneeling to remove the ornate cast-iron hinges. Because the wood was teak, the screws came out smoothly, one by one, but as I knelt there, something else happened: I realized that the last person to turn these screws had been my grandfather, probably kneeling over the cabinet just as I was, and possibly using the same screwdriver. For the first time in my life, the person who had been little more than a photograph on the wall in my dad's study came alive for me, and I felt a deep, almost tangible connection with him. We were bound spiritually over more than 100 years by a common craft and our love for wood.

While Peter's story is about intimate connections that hold families together over generations, lately I've also been thinking about the slaves in your country and ours who developed an extremely high level of skill and artisanry, sometimes bringing these skills across the oceans, as Peter's grandfather did. Many of them used these skills to buy their freedom and became independent craftsmen. Even when I was growing up in Virginia in the fifties, our electrician probably came out of that heritage.

I remember that on one of your visits here we went to Monticello, Thomas Jefferson's home not far from where I grew up. There, we admired the woodwork and, of course, the ingenuity of numerous features in the house. It was clear that many of the artisans who created these things were slaves of this great exponent of human equality. It's only recently that research and documentation has emerged tracing the achievements and the legacy of these usually unknown woodworkers. And the same is true, as I have found out, of the Cape Dutch woodworking at places like Groot Constantia and Boschendal, in your part of the world. While I have all sorts of fancy tools and resources that they didn't have, still, there is a connection of hand and material that links what I am doing in my freedom with what they were doing, often very elegantly, within the brutal and dehumanizing confines of slavery. And sometimes they were doing it to buy their own freedom. There is liberation in this work. The slave artisans in our history help us remember the depths of that claim.

Restoring people who still experience the burdens of these unjust relationships that have shaped the history of your country and mine can take the form of the craft skills that existed even in slavery. I think here again, John, of your work developing the Volmoed Woodworking Co-op with Serghay. Now Anton will be joining you soon on his return from Atlanta, and he has written me about his vision, which seems to dovetail nicely with what you are doing.

> Working in wood has given me so much pleasure over the years and provided such an outlet for my creative drive that I believe it is important to pass the craft on to others, as well as to the next generation. What gives me equal joy is teaching, especially when I can help change a life. I have a vision of helping those who are less fortunate learn new skills, not least using hand tools for those who are looking for something more than working with machines. I see this happening in two ways. The first and primary one would be training people in basic woodworking, enabling them to build items for their own use and also helping them obtain a modest income, maybe through home repairs or construction. The second would be to provide a workshop where those with the necessary desire and ability can make items for sale. The idea here would either be a community style cooperative where workshop space and tools are available for members to use at a small fee, or a production-type shop which employs people.
>
> Besides providing the training needed to make items I would also like to establish a marketing network. I have in mind smaller items such as bar stools, coat racks, coffee tables that can be sold at local markets or through shops. Hopefully this would also lead to commission work for bespoke and other, maybe larger items. I would also like to help teach those interested about related subjects such as finance and marketing.

Now that sounds like a full-scale school evolving here, John. I look forward to the fruition of this dream—as long as you don't fall back into academic administration!

•

No danger, Bill. I have lost my faculties for doing that! But how quickly our time for this conversation has passed. Not that we have run out of subjects to discuss, but I think we better leave our readers time to ruminate and get back to their own shops, whatever they may be. We know, of course, that there is so much more to chat about, and so much more we would like to share with our readers and companions on the journey we continue to travel and enjoy—as well as the legacy we hope to pass on.

But we both know that one mark of a good sermon is to know when to stop. The same is true of writing. And of course, the worst phrase to emerge in our minds when turning a bowl is "just one last cut . . ." How often we have made some foolish mistake at the bench because we went on longer and later than we ought to have done. Maybe that should be our last word of counsel to would-be woodworkers. Don't try and finish something in a hurry; you are bound to make a mistake. Just as there is a rhythm to soul making, so there is to woodworking; rushing a job is not part of that, even if there are deadlines to meet.

We need to call a halt to this conversation, but we do so knowing full well that every day in the workshop we learn something new, our horizons expand, and our friendship deepens. So let's relax in our Adirondack chairs, whether yours or mine, share a glass of Hemel en Aarde wine, or some of your home brew, munch some olives, and continue our conversation in leisure for many years to come! There is more sawdust to make, and the journey of the soul has no end.

A Short Glossary

Every craft, especially an old one, has a virtual dictionary of terms that may confuse or puzzle the outsider. Here are a few terms we used in this book that might need a little definition.

Bandsaw — The bandsaw cuts with a ribbon of teeth on a continuous metal blade driven around a top and bottom wheel through a table where the stock rests. It does not play music, but some large ones are designed to cut meat in a butcher's shop. Make sure you get the right one!

Biscuit (biscuit-joint) — Two pieces of wood are joined with a thin, oval piece of wood (the "biscuit") fitted into matching slots on each piece. Biscuits come in different sizes and even shapes. Not to be consumed while working, or at any other time.

Bit — Any cutting edge rotating on a shaft that is fitted into a drill or router. Not to be confused with a byte.

Brace — A hand-held drilling tool whose shaft is bent to enable the operator to rotate it with increased leverage.

Crosscut — A cut across the grain, hence cross-cut saws.

Dado — A rectangular groove cut in the wood into which a thin panel or tenon can be fitted.

Dovetail (joint) — A fan-shaped end cut into a board so that it can be fitted into a matching notch in the other board, creating a secure joint.

End grain — Speaks for itself! But keep in mind that end grain cannot be securely glued, nor does it take kindly to nails and screws. On fine work it also needs to be hidden unless used as a feature.

Figure — A pattern in the grain of a wood.

Forstner bit — A drill bit with extended cutting edge that creates a flat bottom in the drilled hole.

Fret saw — A hand-held tool shaped like a large "U" with a thin blade attached to the two ends. The scroll saw (also called a jigsaw), a power tool, does the same thing but looks a little like a miniature bandsaw, except it does not have wheels. Instead, the arms holding the blade move rapidly up and down, pushing and pulling its thin blade. Both are very useful for doing fine work, like cutting inlays or small curves.

Gate-leg — A leg to support a table-top that swings out from the main base of the table.

Headstock — The motor-driven end of a lathe, to which the wood is affixed for turning. On some lathes the headstock can be turned at an angle to the bed in order to turn large bowls.

Inlay — Any piece of thin wood, glass, mosaic, or similar material that is fitted into a matching cavity in the wood's surface.

Jig — A device constructed specifically to help with a woodworking operation. While not a dance, woodworking is filled with jigs, many of which are marked and stored . . . somewhere. Great time savers. There are some very helpful books on jig making. Consult the bibliography.

Joinery — The kind of woodworking that involves fastening wood together, as distinguished from most carving or woodturning. Accomplished woodworkers prize their ability to make elegant joints.

Jointer — A power tool with a long flat bed divided into an infeed and outfeed section, on which wood is flattened on one side by passing over revolving blades in the middle. Your fingers should not touch them (or any other blades, come to think of it) unless you are changing them. Make sure you unplug—not just turn off—the machine!

Lathe — A tool that spins a piece of wood at a high speed in order to cut it into a round form with a variety of cutting tools. Spindles are pieces of wood that are turned with the grain running lengthways (e.g., table legs); bowls are mostly turned across the grain.

Mitre — A tool that holds wood to be cut at a fixed angle. Also, the joint created by two woods that have a mitred edge. Not to be confused with a bishop's hat. Mitres can be cut by hand using a mitre-box. Power mitre saws are a brilliant but expensive alternative.

Mortise — A cavity cut into a piece of wood to accept a tenon, creating a strong joint. This is called a mortise and tenon joint. Hence tenon saw. From Latin *tenere*, to hold. Got it?

Planer (*thickness planer*) — A power tool that levels the opposite surfaces of wood so that the wood is of an equal thickness. One side is flattened on a jointer. Then the other side is flattened to an even thickness. Keep your fingers out of them in case you have not yet got the message!

Rip — To cut wood along its grain, hence rip saw. Circular saws do the job these days for most of us.

Router — A machine that accepts a variety of bits to make incisions and cavities in the wood. They may be handheld, and moved over the wood, or fastened under a router table, with the wood passing by the spinning bit. This term was stolen from us by computer geeks.

Spokeshave — A handheld bladed device that is drawn over a piece of wood to shape it to a desired curve or flatness.

Template — A piece of wood cut to a desired shape to guide a saw or router to make identical pieces.

Bibliography

Sources for Reflection

Arendt, Hannah. *The Human Condition*. Chicago: University of Chicago Press, 1958.

Clement, Mark. *The Carpenter's Notebook*. Arlington, VA: CenterLine, 2005.

Cook, Roger. *The Tree of Life: Image for the Cosmos*. London: Thames and Hudson, 1988.

Craft Art and Religion: Second International Seminar. Rome: Vatican, 1978.

Crawford, Matthew B. *Shop Class as Soulcraft: An Inquiry into the Value of Work*. New York: Penguin, 2009.

de Gruchy, John W. *Confessions of a Christian Humanist*. Minneapolis: Fortress, 2006.

———. *Led Into Mystery: Faith Seeking Answers in Life and Death*. London: SCM, 2013.

———. "Retrieving the Soul: Understanding the Soul as Complex, Dynamic and Relational." *Journal of Theology in Southern Africa* 149 (July 2014) 56–69.

Dustin, Chris, and Joanna Ziegler. *Practicing Mortality*. London: Palgrave Macmillan, 2007. (See especially chapter 5, "A Reverence for Wood.")

Emery, Olivia H. *Craftsman Lifestyle: The Gentle Revolution*. Pasadena, CA: California Design Publications, 1978.

Everett, William J. *The Politics of Worship: Reforming the Language and Symbols of Liturgy*. Cleveland, OH: United Church Press, 1999. (Revised edition available free at www.WilliamEverett.com as *Praying for God's Republic: A Proposal for Transforming our Worship*.)

———. "With the Grain: Woodworking, Spirituality, and the Struggle for Justice." *The Journal of Theology for Southern Africa* 123 (Nov 2005) 6–15.

King, Stephen. *On Writing: A Memoir of the Craft*. New York: Pocket Books, 2001.

Krenov, James. *A Cabinetmaker's Notebook*. 1976. Reprint. Fresno, CA: Linden, 2000.

———. *With Wakened Hands: Furniture by James Krenov and Students*. Fresno, CA: Cambium, 2000.

Laird, Ross A. *Grain of Truth: The Ancient Lessons of Craft*. New York: Walker and Co., 2001.

Maloof, Sam. *Sam Maloof: Woodworker*. Tokyo: Kodansha Institute, 1983.

Nakashima, George. *The Soul of a Tree*. 1981. Reprint. Tokyo: Kodansha International, 1988.

Osolnik, Rude. *A Life Turning Wood*. Louisville: Crescent Hill, 1997.

Pakenham, Thomas. *Meetings with Remarkable Trees*. Johannesburg: Jonathan Ball, 1996.

———. *Remarkable Trees of the World*. London: Weidenfeld & Nicolson, 2002.

Paz, Octavio. *In Praise of Hands: Contemporary Crafts of the World*. Greenwich, CT: New York Graphic Society, 1974. (Especially the section on "Use and Contemplation.")

Polkinghorne, John. "Eschatological Credibility: Emergent and Teleological Processes." In *Resurrection: Theological and Scientific Assessments*, edited by Robert John Russell, Ted Peters, and Michael Welker, 43–55. Grand Rapids: Eerdmans, 2002.

Pye, David. *The Nature and Art of Workmanship*. Bethel, CT: Cambium, 1995.

Sennett, Richard. *The Craftsman*. New Haven: Yale University Press, 2008.

Sloane, Eric. *A Reverence for Wood*. New York: Ballantine, 1965.

Wearing, Robert. *The Resourceful Woodworker*. London: Batsforth, 1991.

Winnicott, Donald. *Playing and Reality*. London: Tavistock, 1971.

History

Boris, Eileen. *Art and Labor: Ruskin, Morris, and the Craftsman Ideal in America*. Philadelphia: Temple University Press, 1986.

The Craftsman in America. Washington, DC: National Geographic Society, 1975.

Green, Harvey. *Wood: Craft, Culture, History*. London: Penguin, 2006.

Kaplan, Wendy. *"The Art that is Life": The Arts and Crafts Movement in America, 1875–1920*. Boston: Museum of Fine Arts, 1987.

Landow, George P. *The Aesthetic and Critical Theories of John Ruskin*. Princeton: Princeton University Press, 1971.

Lemire, Eugene D., ed. *The Unpublished Lectures of William Morris*. Detroit: Wayne State University Press, 1969.

Logan, William Bryant. *Oak: The Frame of Civilization*. New York and London: Norton, 2005.

MacCarthy, Fiona. *William Morris: A Life for our Time*. New Edition. London: Faber and Faber, 2003.

Marshall, Roderick. *William Morris and the Earthly Paradise*. Tisbury, UK: Compton, 1979.

Sprigg, June, and David Larkin. *Shaker Life, Work, and Art*. New York: Stewart, Tabonic, and Change, 1987.

Manuals and How-to Books

Abram, Norm. *Measure Twice, Cut Once: Lessons from a Master Carpenter*. Boston: Little, Brown, 1996.

Boase, Tony. *Bowl Turning Techniques Master Class*. Lewes, East Sussex, UK: Guild of Mastercraftsman, 1991.

Edlin, Herbert. *What Wood Is That? A Manual of Wood Identification*. London: Thames and Hudson, 1969.

Flexner, Bob. *Understanding Wood Finishing*. Pleasantville, NY: Readers' Digest, 1994.

Kemner, Paul, and Peggy Zdila, *Building Arts and Crafts Furniture*. New York: Sterling, 1997.

Korn, Peter. *Working with Wood: The Basics of Craftmanship.* Newtown, CT: Taunton, 1993.

Raffan, Richard. *Turning Wood.* Newtown, CT: Taunton, 1985.

————. *Shop-made Jigs & Fixtures.* Alexandria, VA: Time-Life, 1994.

Simpson, Chris. *The Essential Guide to Woodwork.* London: Murdoch, 2001.

————. *The Encyclopedia of Wood.* Foreword by John Makepeace. New York: Facts on File, 1989.

Magazines

American Woodturner (Journal of the American Association of Woodturners). The basic resource for woodturners, at www.woodturner.org.

British Woodworking. Freshwood Publishing. The UK's No. 1 woodworking magazine, at www.britishwoodworking.com.

Fine Woodworking. Published by the Taunton Press, source of many excellent materials on woodworking, at www.finewoodworking.com.

About the Authors

William J. Everett grew up in and around Washington, DC, with further education at Wesleyan University, Yale Divinity School, and Harvard University. With his advanced degrees in Christian social ethics, he then taught for over thirty years, first in Milwaukee, WI, at St. Francis Seminary, then in Atlanta at Emory University's Candler School of Theology, and finally in the Boston area at Andover Newton Theological School, before retiring in 2001 to focus on writing and woodworking. Sabbaticals took him to guest teaching in Heidelberg and Frankfurt, Germany; Bangalore, India; and Cape Town, South Africa.

He has written extensively on church and society issues involving family, economics, ecology, politics, symbolism, and law. Earlier works include *God's Federal Republic: Reconstructing Our Governing Symbol*, and *Religion, Federalism, and the Struggle for Public Life: Cases from Germany, India, and America*. His book, *The Politics of Worship* laid the groundwork for current projects of roundtable worship and conversation circles. After retiring, he turned to fiction writing and poetry, with the publication in 2008 of *Red Clay, Blood River*, a story told by Earth of connections between America's Trail of Tears and South Africa's Great Trek. This was followed by a collection of poems, *Turnings: Poems of Transformation*. In addition to his poetry writing, he is currently doing research for a projected book about his grandfather's mining work on Cyprus in the 1920s. Pictures, downloads, and commentary about his work can be found at his website www.WilliamEverett.com, where he blogs regularly.

Bill lives in Waynesville, NC, with his wife Sylvia Johnson Everett, an artist in fabric, mosaics, paper, and found materials. Her works have been exhibited in the US, Germany, and South Africa. For more about Bill and Sylvia's work visit their gallery at www.WisdomsTable.net.

John W. de Gruchy was born in Pretoria, South Africa, in March 1939. He studied at the University of Cape Town, Rhodes University, Chicago Theological Seminary and the University of Chicago, and at the University of South Africa. An ordained minister in the United Congregational Church, he served two congregations before joining the staff of the South African Council of Churches in 1968, where he was director of Communications and Studies. In 1973 he was appointed to the faculty of the University of Cape Town, where he eventually became the Robert Selby Taylor Professor of Christian Studies and, during the last few years of his tenure, the Director of the Graduate School in Humanities. He retired in 2003 and was appointed a Senior Research Scholar at UCT and an Extraordinary Professor at the University of Stellenbosch, and remains active in both institutions, engaged in research, publishing, and mentoring.

With his wife Isobel—a painter, poet, botanist, and mathematician—he is now a resident member of the Volmoed Community for Reconciliation and Healing, near Hermanus, where he writes, gives seminars, and makes furniture. A frequent lecturer around the globe and recipient of several honorary doctorates, he is a prolific author. Among his books are *The Church Struggle in South Africa; Christianity and Democracy; Christianity, Art and Social Transformation; Reconciliation: Restoring Justice; Being Human: Confessions of a Christian Humanist;* and *Led into Mystery.*

Manufactured by Amazon.ca
Bolton, ON

An American ethicist and a South African theologian reflect on their wor
with wood and how it has helped them find creativity and meaning in experiences o
both loss and transformation. Through their friendship, correspondence, and work
together they have developed a rich narrative about the way this craftwork has shap
their relationships with family, friends, and the natural environment. Their conve
sation invites both craftspeople and religious seekers to join them on a spiritua
journey toward fresh insight and inspiration.

"The title and subtitle are exactly right. This is 'A Conversation about Woodworkin
and Spirituality' in which 'sawdust flies in all directions, but the soul also takes
wings.' So, reader, prepare to pause often to reflect on your own life journey as yo
listen to Everett's and de Gruchy's. This is wisdom beautifully communicated. The
added poetry, illustrations, and photos only enhance it."

—Larry Rasmussen
Reinhold Niebuhr Professor Emeritus of Social Ethics, Union Theological Seminary, New York City, NY

"This absorbing and often moving conversation about friendship, faith, and the woo
worker's craft invites us to explore the inner journeys that accompany the workir
and shaping of wood. The obvious joy of the authors in their soul-deepening craft
will strike an immediate chord with fellow woodworkers—and invite some who hav
not yet felt the warm texture of newly planed wood grain under their fingers to go
out and buy their first tools."

—Peter Storey
Distinguished Professor Emeritus of the Practice of Christian Ministry, Duke Divinity School, Durham,

"In *Sawdust and Soul*, I felt like I was standing across a workbench from two friend
reminiscing, philosophizing, and reflecting about woodworking, the influence it ha
on their lives and their relationship. The journey I experienced with Bill and John
resonates with my own."

—Gregory Paolini
Director of Operations, Gregory Paolini Design LLC, World Class Woodworking, Canton, NC

William J. Everett taught Christian ethics in graduate schools for over th
before turning to woodworking. In addition to his academic books and articles,
author of *Red Clay, Blood River*, an eco-historical novel, as well as *Turnings*, a cc
his poetry. He lives in the hardwood forest of western North Carolina with his wif
liturgical artist in many media.

One of South Africa's most celebrated theologians, **John W. de Gruch**
woodworker, with pieces in many churches, schools, and homes throughout the coun
and abroad. Among his recent books are *Confessions of a Christian Humanist* and *L*
into Mystery. He and his wife, Isobel, are members of the Volmoed Christian Commun
near Hermanus, South Africa, where he writes, gives seminars, and does woodworking, wl
Isobel paints and writes poetry.

Religion / Spirituality

Cover Art: "Shrine" by William J. Everett
www.wipfandstock.com

Cascade Books
An Imprint of WIPF and STOCK Publishers

$3.99

ISBN 978-1-62564-46
9 781625 644463